GARMENT PAT...
1889
with INSTRUCTIONS

edited by Jules & Kaethe Kliot

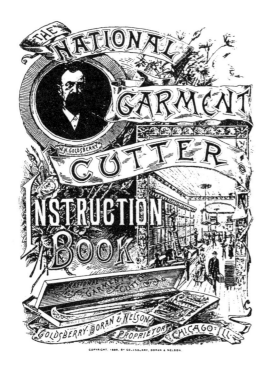

LACIS
PUBLICATIONS

The work of this book is taken, essentially unabridged, from:

THE NATIONAL GARMENT CUTTER INSTRUCTION BOOK by Goldsberry, Doran & Nelson published in 1889

     and

THE NATIONAL GARMENT CUTTER BOOK OF DIAGRAMS by Goldsberry, Doran & Nelson published in 1889

This volume includes patterns for over 75 everyday garments for men women and children including street costume, undergarments, overalls, aprons, wraps and capes. The presentation of patterns is typical of this period, when most garments were individually made by the trained home sewer or professional tailor. The full size, sized tissue paper patterns would soon replace these quarterly publications and the standardization of sizes would lead to the popularity of ready-to-wear clothing , a major marketing trend by 1910.

Reprinted from the trade periodical The National Garment Cutter. the patterns are to scale and can be enlarged by lens, grid or measurement, following the dimensions shown on the drawing, and then adjusted to actual body measurements. Instructions for fitting to body measurements and use of French curves are included

ECCENTRICITIES OF FASHION IN HIGH LIFE.

1. Candlestick Hat with Cat and Mice Accompaniment. 2. The same, tilted à la Hussar. 3. Loaf-shaped Hat with Doves and Peacock-tail Brim, fantastic Dress to match. 4. à la Coachman, with Bird-nest Trimming. 5. Waddling Duck and old Woman looking out of Tower. 6, 7, 8. Procession of Costumes with Tournures more or less pronounced. 9. Dress à la high-backed Chair.

HARPER'S BAZAR, April 18, 1985

LACIS
PUBLICATIONS
3163 Adeline Street, Berkeley, CA 94703

© 1996, LACIS
ISBN 0-916896-74-9

COVER ILL: *HARPER'S BAZAR, March 27, 1986*

INTRODUCTION

Womens' fashions of the 1880's, dominated by the large bustle, must surely represent one of the most grotesque styles and images created by man. It was a period when the cartoon became reality, when the subtle bustle made of horsehair in the 1870's now expanded, with the help of great mechanical supports which could rise and collapse as necessary for such basic activities as sitting and standing, to the immense shelves so typical of the late 1880's. The engineering and mechanics of these devices were surely an outgrowth of the mechanical age, which made possible this awkward, unbalanced new aesthetic. The irony of this contorted silhouette being accepted during a period when women's liberation was becoming a major social issue might only represent a final fruitless effort by the Paris designers to obviate their power. Reality would soon take hold and what took 30 years to develop, virtually disappeared overnight. By 1890, the bustle was no more, and the new lines of the large sleeves and narrow waist would prevail.

CONTENTS

YOUNG LADIES JOURNAL, December 1988

HARPER'S BAZAR, April 18, 1985

HARPER'S BAZAR, March 27, 1986

HARPER'S BAZAR, April 18, 1985

HARPER'S BAZAR, April 18, 1985

4

YOUNG LADIES JOURNAL, December 1988

General Directions.

The set is composed of a book, a set of scales, a folding square, curved pieces or scroll, tape measure and tracing wheel.

All garments here given are drafted upon the same general plan of work.

BEFORE MAKING A DRAFT of any kind the special directions should be read, as it will often save a great deal of trouble, and probably prevent the draft from being made wrong.

THE INSTRUCTIONS in the first basque should be very carefully studied by the beginner before trying to cut any other garment.

No thoughtful person will attempt making even the first draft without reading and carefully studying the instructions there given if it is their first work.

It will save much valuable time and make them much more efficient, besides saving their teachers telling them repeatedly what is told there plainly.

The first important step is taking the measures, and no one can get a correct fit of a garment from improper measures.

TO TAKE MEASURES. (Illustrated on third page.) Great care should be taken in getting measures.

TAKE BUST MEASURE with the tape measure straight around the largest part of the bust as shown on third page, high up under the arms; take snug, close measure, neither too tight nor too loose.

TAKE MEASURE AROUND THE WAIST as tight as the dress is to be worn.

TAKE LENGTH OF WAIST from the large joint, where neck and body join, down to the waist. Care must be taken to get this measure.

SLEEVE MEASURE is taken from the center of back to wrist joint with arm raised and elbow bent.

IN CUTTING a garment look carefully at the draft being copied; use numbers and curves as shown in draft.

IF THE BEGINNERS will study the drafts in the first basque here given until they understand the principles, they will have no trouble whatever, but if they skip around from draft to draft without mastering any of them, it will take more time and worry to understand the work than is necessary. By noticing each line drawn before trying to draw, it will make easy work. Draw all straight lines with the square, all curved lines with the curved drafting tool.

THE ARROWS are used for two purposes: One to show which way to turn the curve the other the number of points to be connected with the curve.

THE CURVE should always be turned with the largest part in the direction in which the arrow points. The letter A in corner of a draft is the starting point in making draft. A careful study of these directions, together with the special directions given, will enable any person with average intelligence to use the work without any personal teaching. Learn to cut the first basque here given, and the problem is solved. Practice makes perfect in this as well as in anything else.

The instructions in all drafts, after the first basque, are made as brief as possible, as the plan of work is the same in all and no need to repeat.

The instructions in making up the garments apply only to special features, as the instructions in book accompanying the Garment Cutter go into detail on that subject; hence it is useless to repeat the general plan here as to joining the parts found in every garment.

There are many times a lady can make up a combination suit by using the parts that are good of two or even more of her dresses that are par-tially worn. The style this season permits it, in fact encourages it; as well it should, as it combines both beauty and economy. It is the same in chil-dren's clothing.

In making these combinations often a pleasant result is obtained in using parts of different drafts. That is to say, the back of one and the front of another, etc.

In such cases care must be taken to put the different parts together, so that seam lines, waist lines, etc., come out properly.

In conclusion, we must repeat most emphatic-ally: Master the first drafts before going a step farther.

7

LADIES' PLAIN COSTUME.

THE BASQUE.

Is in 6 pieces: Front, Back, Side Back, Collar and two Sleeve portions.

Read instructions carefully before making draft.

In the first place, take the bust measure with the tape measure straight around the largest part of the bust, and as high up under the arm as can conveniently be done, drawing the tape measure moderately tight, and write the result on a card (or slip of paper).

Get the length of the back next; take the tape measure, place it at the large joint in back of neck where neck and body join, passing it down to the waist. If it is difficult to determine just where the waist line should be located, tie a string or belt around the waist just as far down as the waist can be worn; by this means you can obtain the correct measure, or length of waist, and write this result on the card.

Get the waist measure next; put the tape measure around the waist, and draw it as tight as can conveniently be drawn, and put this result on the card.

Get the length of the sleeve next; raise the arm, bend the elbow and measure from the center of back, and put this result on the card also.

Now we have all the measures required to cut a basque.

The backs of all waists are always drafted first.

After obtaining the bust measure, select the corresponding scale and place it on the long arm of the square and proceed; first place the square on paper and draw a base line, and also draw a short line at the top of the square, to form a square as shown in figure 1.

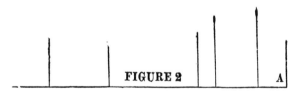

FIGURE 1

Then proceed to get the figures on the base line, beginning at the upper right hand corner of draft; the first figure from the top is $\frac{1}{2}$; then make a point at $\frac{1}{2}$ on the paper; the next is $2\frac{3}{8}$ make a point also; the next is 6, next $10\frac{1}{4}$. As our scales are but 10 spaces long, make an X at the end of the scale (or even with the 10 on the scale), and move the square down even with the X, and make a point at $\frac{1}{4}$; that gives us $10\frac{1}{4}$. The next is 15; this is the waist line. Make an X even with the figure 10, and move square down even with the X, as before. Now we have 20 spaces. The next figure is 22. Make a point at 2, and that gives you 22. The next is $22\frac{1}{2}$.

Now we have all the points on the outside of the base line.

Now proceed to get width, on cross measure lines, as shown in figure 2.

FIGURE 2   A

Place the scale on the short arm of the square and place the square at the top of the draft. Care should be taken to keep the square perfectly straight on the base line.

The first figure on the top cross measure line is $2\frac{3}{8}$; make a point and move the square down to first cross line (omitting $\frac{1}{2}$ on base line, as there is no cross line drawn from it), making a point at 6 and draw a line to base line. Move the square down to the second cross line; make a point at $5\frac{3}{4}$ and draw line to base line. Move the square down to the third cross line, making points at $\frac{1}{4}$ and $3\frac{7}{8}$ and draw line as before; then move square down to the fourth cross line (or waist line), and make a point at $\frac{1}{2}$ and $2\frac{3}{4}$, and draw a line. Move the square down to fifth cross line and make a point at $4\frac{3}{4}$, and draw a line to base line. As we now have all the points, we will proceed to get out lines with the curve.

The curve is laid on the diagram in the different forms. Each curve has an arrow on it pointing to the largest part of the curve. Bear this in mind, as all the diagrams in the following pages have arrows to show which way to lay the curve. We draft the neck first. Lay the curve on points $2\frac{3}{8}$ on top cross measure line and $\frac{1}{2}$ on base line and draw a line.

Draw the shoulder next. Connect points $2\frac{3}{8}$ on top cross line and 6 on first cross line.

The next is the arm size. Connect point 6 on first cross line and $5\frac{3}{4}$ on second cross line (this is the only instance where the small part of the curve is used.) Draw the curved line from arm size to waist line by connecting points $5\frac{3}{4}$ on second cross line and $3\frac{7}{8}$ on third cross line, move curve down to points $3\frac{7}{8}$ on third cross line and $2\frac{3}{4}$ on fourth cross line (or waist line), then turn curve over and connect points $2\frac{3}{4}$ on waist line and $4\frac{3}{4}$ on fifth cross line. If the hips are very large give more spring with the curve. Now shape the bottom of the basque by connecting points $4\frac{3}{4}$ on fifth cross line and $22\frac{1}{2}$ on base line. Get the curve in center of back by connecting points $\frac{1}{2}$ on fourth cross line or waist line and $\frac{1}{4}$ on third cross line, turn the curve over and connect points $\frac{1}{4}$ on third cross line and $\frac{1}{2}$ on base line, then go down to the waist line and connect points $\frac{1}{2}$ anb $22\frac{1}{2}$ on base line.

This completes the draft for the back. Draft the side back next.

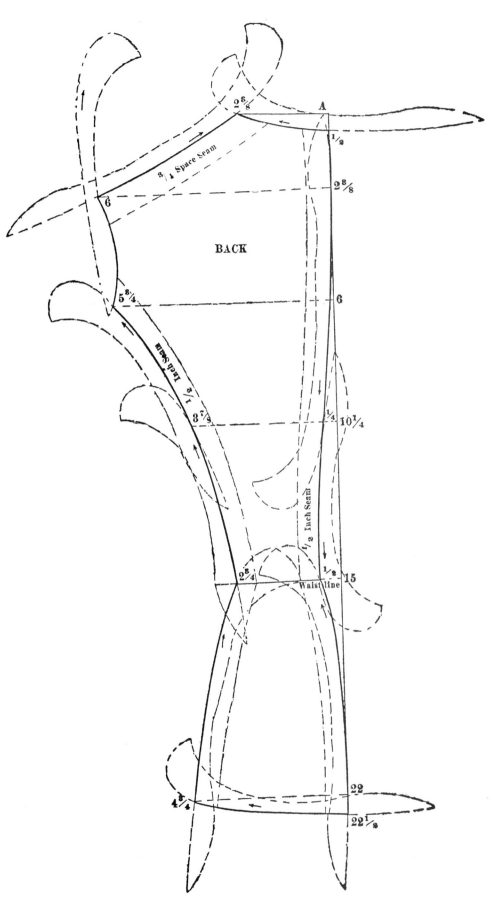

9

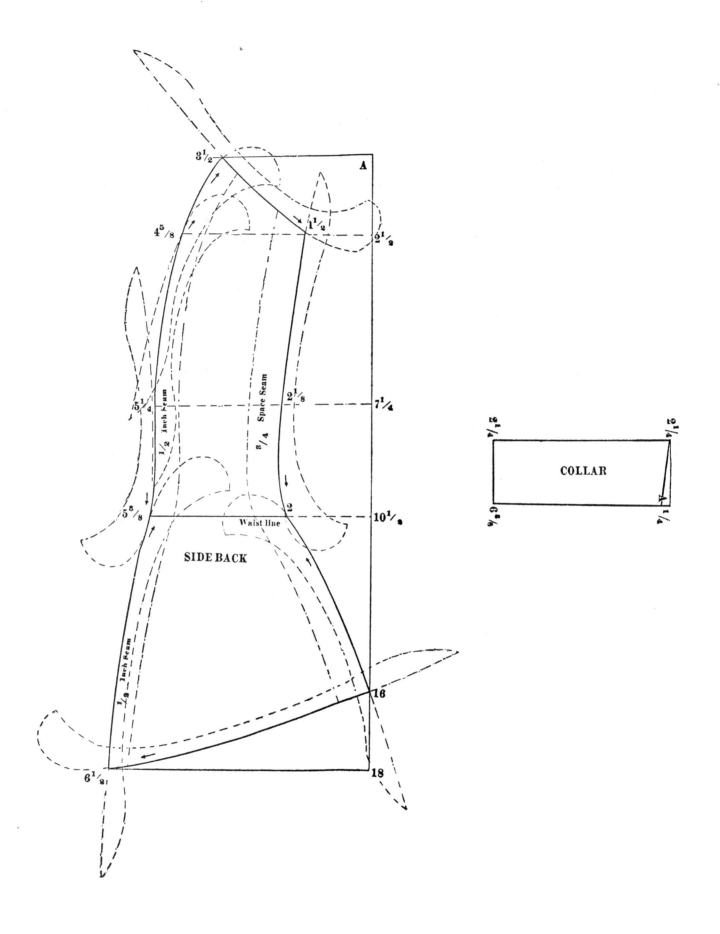

3½

A

4⅝

1½

2½

5¼

½ Inch Seam

Space Seam

¾

2⅛

7¼

5⅝

2

Waist line

10½

SIDE BACK

½ Inch Seam

16

6½

18

COLLAR

2¼

2¼

6¾

A

¼

10

LADIES' PLAIN COSTUME.—Continued.

THE SIDE BACK.

Use the same scale and draft the side back upon the same plan as the back.

First square the paper by drawing the base line; then proceed to get the points. The first figure down is $2\frac{1}{2}$, make a point; the next is $7\frac{1}{4}$, make a point; the next is $10\frac{1}{2}$, make an X at the 10 on the scale, and move square down even with the X and make a point at $\frac{1}{2}$, this gives us $10\frac{1}{2}$. This is the waist line. The next is 16, make a point; the next is 18, make a point.

These are all the figures or points on the outside of base line. Now proceed to get the width or cross lines.

Put the scale on the short arm of the square as before. The first figure is $3\frac{1}{2}$ on top measure line. Make a point at $1\frac{1}{2}$ and $4\frac{5}{8}$, draw a line to base line. Move square down to second cross line, make a point at $2\frac{1}{8}$ and $5\frac{1}{4}$ and draw line; then move square down to the third cross line (or waist line), and make a point at 2 and $5\frac{3}{8}$, draw line to base line. Move square down to bottom line (omitting point 16 on base line as there is no cross line drawn from it), and make a point at $6\frac{1}{2}$ and draw line to base line.

Now we have all the points, and we will proceed to get the outline, with the curve.

First connect points $3\frac{1}{2}$ on top cross line and $1\frac{1}{2}$ on first cross line, draw a line; then connect points $3\frac{1}{2}$ on top cross line and $4\frac{5}{8}$ on first cross line, move curve down and connect points $4\frac{5}{8}$ on first cross line, and $5\frac{1}{4}$ on second cross line. Reverse the curve and turn it over, and connect $5\frac{1}{4}$ on second cross line, and $5\frac{3}{8}$ on third cross line (or waist line). Reverse the curve again and turn it over, and connect points $5\frac{3}{8}$ on waist line and $6\frac{1}{2}$ on bottom line. Then shape the bottom by connecting points $6\frac{1}{2}$ on bottom line and 16 on base line; then go to the waist line and connect points 2 on waist line and $2\frac{1}{8}$ an second cross line and $1\frac{1}{2}$ on first cross line, draw from the three points at once, then go back to waist line, reversing curve turn it over, and connect points 2 on waist line and 16 on base line.

This completes the draft for the side back.

Draft the front next.

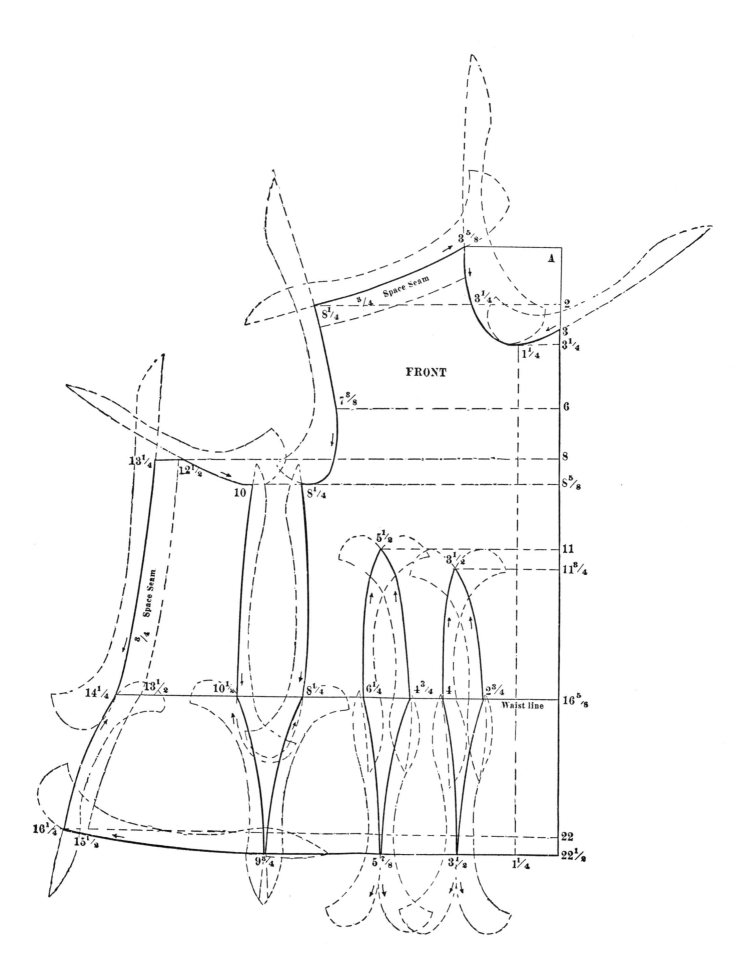

12

LADIES' PLAIN COSTUME.—Continued.

THE FRONT.

Use same scale as for back and side back; draft upon the same plan.

First square the paper, then proceed to get the points on the base line; the first figure down is 2, make a point; the next is 3, make a point; next 3¼, make a point; the next is 6, make a point; the next is 8, make a point; next 8⅝, make a point; the next is 11, make an X at the 10, and move square down as before, and make a point at 1, that gives us 11; next 11¾, make a point; the next is 16⅝, make a point—this is the waist line; the next is 22, make an X at the 10 on scale, and move square down as before, and make a point at 2, that gives us 22, the next is 22½; make a point. This is all the points on the outside of base line. Now proceed as before to get the width, or cross measure lines.

The first is 3⅝ on top measure line, make a point; move square down to first cross line and make point at 3¼ and 8¼, and draw line to base line; then move square down to second cross line (omitting the point 3 on base line, as there is no cross line drawn from it), and make a point at 1¼ and draw line, move square down to third cross line and make point at 7⅝, draw line; move square down to fourth cross line and make X at end of scale, but before moving out to make the points, draw a line the length of the short arm, which enables us to to keep the line square; then move the square even with the X and proceed as before; make a point at 2½ and 3¼, which gives us 12½ and 13¼; then move square down to fifth cross line and make a point at 8¼ and 10 (do not make a cross at 10 when it occurs on the diagram as this one does); then move square down to sixth cross line and make point at 5½ and draw line; move square down to seventh cross line and make point at 3½ and draw line, then move square down to eighth cross line, or waist line, and make points at 2¾ and 4, and 4¾ and 6¼, and 8¼ and 10½, and 13½ and 14¼, draw line as above; move square down to ninth cross line and make point at 15½ and 16¼, and draw line as above; then move square down to bottom line and make points 1¼ and 3½, and 5⅝ and 9¾, draw line to base line. Now we have all the points, and proceed as before to get the outlines with the curve.

Draw the neck first by connecting points 3⅝ on top measure line, and 3¼ on first cross line, and 1¼ on second cross line; draw from the three points at once; then reverse the curve and connect points 1¼ on second cross line and 3 on base line.

Draw the shoulder next; connect points 3⅝ on top measure line, and 8¼ on first cross line; then reverse the curve and draw the arm size; connect points 8¼ on first cross line and 7⅝ on third cross line; and 8¼ on fifth cross line; draw from the three points at once; reverse the curve and connect points 10 on fifth cross line and 12½ on fourth cross line; then connect points 13¼ on fourth cross line and 14¼ on eighth cross line (or waist line); then reverse the curve and turn it over and connect points 14¼ on the waist line and 16¼ on ninth cross line; then shape the bottom by connecting points 16¼ on ninth cross line and 9¾ on the bottom line.

Now we will draw the darts. Draw the under-arm dart first; connect points 10 on fifth cross line and 10½ on waist line and draw a line; turn the curve over and connect points 8¼ on fifth cross line and 8¼ on waist line, and draw line; reverse the curve and draw from 8¼ on waist line to 9¾ on the bottom line; turn the curve over and connect points 10½ on waist line and 9¾ on bottom line; now draw the front darts, connect points 5½ on sixth cross line and 6¼ on waist line; draw line, turn the curve over and draw line from 5½ on sixth cross line 4¾ on waist line, reverse the curve and proceed as above.

The front dart is gotten in the same way.

The dotted line from 1¼ on second cross line and 1¼ on the bottom line is for the hem.

This completes the front

Draft the sleeves next.

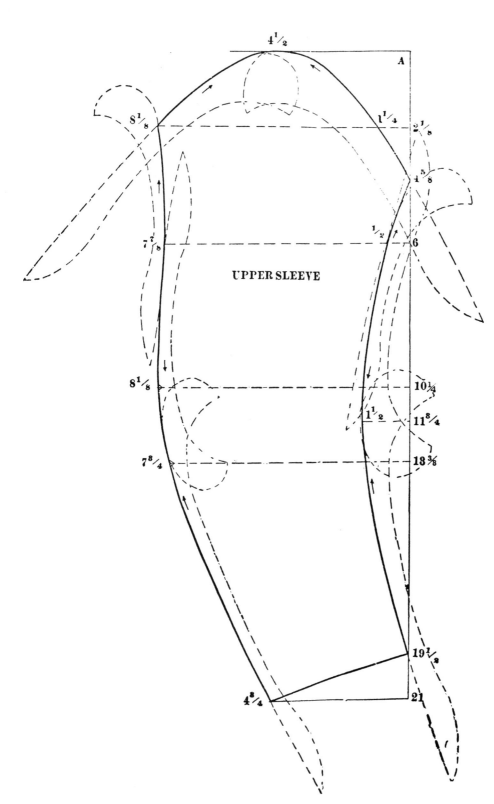

LADIES' PLAIN COSTUME.—Continued.

UPPER SLEEVE.

Use the same scale as for Front back and Side back and draft upon the same plan. Draft the upper part of Sleeve first, square the paper as before and proceed to get the points.

The first figure down is $2\frac{1}{8}$, make point; the next is $4\frac{5}{8}$, make point; the next is 6, make point, the next is $10\frac{1}{4}$, make point, the next is $11\frac{3}{4}$, make an X at the end of scale (or even with the 10 on scale) and move the square down even with the X as before, and make point at $1\frac{3}{4}$, and that give $11\frac{3}{4}$.

The next is $13\frac{3}{8}$, make a point; the next is $19\frac{1}{2}$, make point: the next is 21, make an X at end of scale and move square down as above and make point at 1, that gives us 21. Now we have all the figures or points on the outside of the base line.

Now proceed to get the cross measure lines. Put the scale on the short arm of the square. The first figure is $4\frac{1}{2}$ on top measure line, make point: move the square down to first cross line and make point at $1\frac{1}{4}$ and $8\frac{1}{8}$ and draw line to base line. Move scale down to second cross line (omitting the figure $4\frac{5}{8}$ on base line as there is no cross line drawn from it), make point at $\frac{1}{2}$ and $7\frac{7}{8}$, draw line. Move square down to third cross line and make point at $8\frac{1}{8}$. Draw line to base line. Move square down to the fourth cross line and make point at $1\frac{1}{2}$, draw line. Move

square down to fifth cross
line, and make point at 7¾,
draw line. Move square
down to bottom line (omitting 19½ on base line) and
make point at 4¾ and draw
line to base line.

Now we have all the
points. We proceed to
get the outlines with the
curve. First draw the top
by connecting points 4½ on
top cross measure line and
1¼ on first cross measure
line and 4⅝ on base line.
Draw from the three points
at once. Turn the curve
over and connect points 4½
on top measure line and 8⅛
on first cross line Then
connect points 8⅛ on first
cross line and 7⅞ on second
cross line. Reverse the
curve and draw from 7⅞ on
second cross line and 8⅛ on
third cross line. Reverse
the curve again and connect
points 7¾ on fifth cross line
and 4¾ on the bottom line.
Now draw the inside line
by connecting points 4⅝ on
base line and ½ on second
cross line. Reverse curve
and connect points ½ on second cross line and 1½ on
fourth cross line. Reverse
curve again and connect
points 1½ on fourth cross
line and 19½ on base line.
Draw a straight line from 4¾
on the bottom line to 19½ on
base line.

We deem it unnecessary
to describe the under part
of the sleeve. You connect
three points by drawing a
line from 4½ on top measure
line and 1½ on first cross line
and 1½ on base line. This
completes the basque.

Learn to master this
before going farther.

Three-eighth inch seams
are allowed on the sleeves.

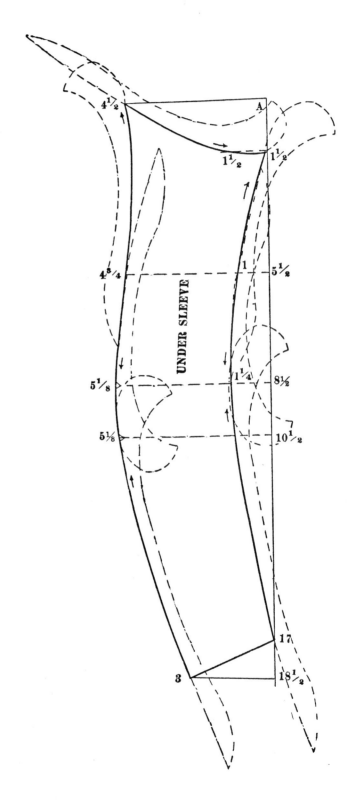

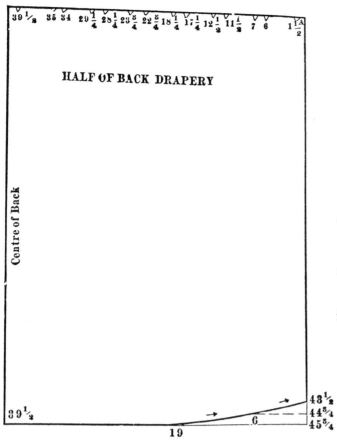

HALF OF BACK DRAPERY

Centre of Back

39½ 35 34 29¼ 25¼ 23⅝ 22⅝ 18½ 17¼ 12½ 11½ 7 6 1 A/2

39½

43½
44¾
45¾

19   6

LADIES' PLAIN COSTUME—Continued.

PLAIN SKIRT.

Use scale corresponding with the waist measure.

Is in three pieces: Front, Back and Side Gore.

This is drafted upon the general plan of the work. The arrows show which way to lay the curve.

Regulate the length by the use of the tape measure.

Now this finishes our first costume. All costumes in the succeeding pages are drafted in like manner.

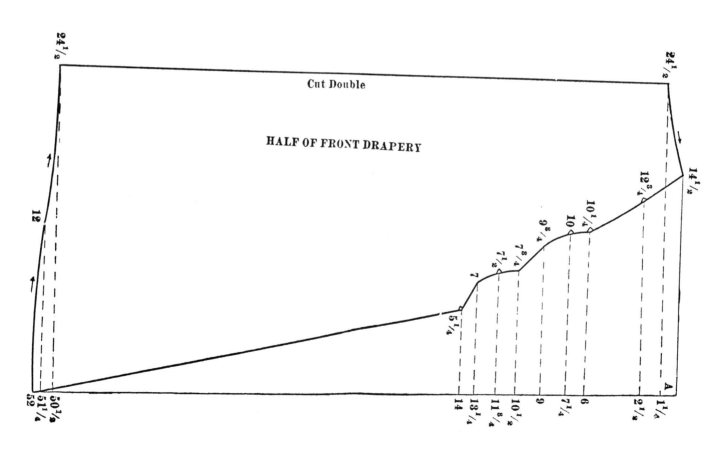

Cut Double

HALF OF FRONT DRAPERY

24½   24½

14½

12¾

1   10¼

12   10

9¾

7¾

7½

7

5¼

52
51¼
50½   14 13¼ 11¾ 10½ 9 7¼ 6 2½ 1¼ A

LADIES' PLAIN SKIRT.

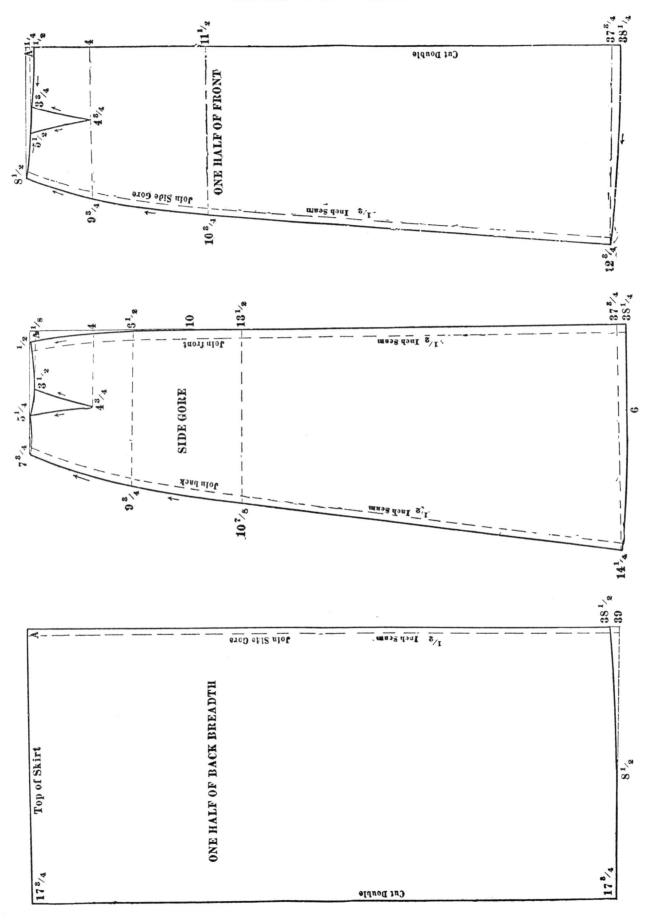

TO CHANGE WAIST LINES.

The back must be drafted first, and where the scale does not bring out the desired length we raise or lower the waist line to the desired length.

Now, supposing we were drafting a waist for a lady, that her measure were as follows:

Bust measure 33
Length of Waist 15½
Around Waist 24
Length of Sleeve 28

Now draft the back first, as has been explained.

Take the draft we have been working on (or any other), but we will take this one.

Make a point at all the figures on base line until we come down to 15; now make a small dot at 15. Take the tape measure and measure from ½ on draft down to 15½, tape line measurement, for that is the length of the lady's waist we are drafting for now; make the point at 15½, tape line measure, instead of 15 scale measure, and notice the difference between the small dot you have made and the point; you can see you have shortened the waist ½ space.

Now draw the waist line at the point instead of at the dot, and raise or lower all lines below the waist line the same distance as waist line.

Change the waist line on front and side back same as on back, but use the scale you are drafting by instead of tape measure.

Now we have shortened the waist ½ space. We lengthen the waist on the same plan. Draw the outlines same as if waist had not been changed.

All seams are ½ inch tape measure, excepting shoulder seams and where sideback and front joins, which are ¾ space (of scale being used).

TO TEST LENGTH OF SLEEVE.

Take measure from centre of back of wrist, deduct width of back piece of garment, being cut minus one inch for seams. Then you will get exact length of sleeve. Measure from top of sleeve to point marked 21 on base line; make the point 21 to correspond with tape measure by raising or lowering it. Raise or lower point marked 19½

same distance. If these points be changed, raise or lower elbow line marked 11¾ half the distance. Change under arm part of sleeve by raising or lowering the wrist and elbow line same distance as in upper part. Same rule applies to all sleeves.

TO TEST SIZE OF WAIST.

Before drawing under arm dart lines, mark off hem on front by connecting point 1¼ (at neck), with point 1¼ on bottom line with straight line.

Then lay off seam on front next to side back, which is ¾ of a space, making precisely the same curves as in outer lines; then mark ¾ of a space seam on side back, next to front, and draw lines as outer lines.

Now measure ½ an inch seam with tape line on side back next to back, and draw lines as outer lines and ½ inch seam on each side of back and draw line same as outer lines.

Then before drawing the under arm dart lines measure net goods across the pattern, on waist line, omitting all seams, darts and hems. If this measure is exact size of waist measure, the measure is correct.

If the measure is not the exact size, the under arm dart must be changed to the desired size.

This is done by moving dart and seam lines at dart in or out one-half the amount that the garment must be changed. In the case of our supposed measure, the waist will be one inch too large. Change the size by moving the dart and seam points of under arm dart ½ inch further apart, or each side ¼ of an inch. The goods being cut double, this will give exact size of waist. Now draw dart line and your pattern is complete.

If the garment had been one inch too small, the points would have been moved one-half inch nearer together, instead of farther apart.

If it had been two inches too small, one-half that amount would be an inch, consequently we would have to meet the points one inch nearer together, or one-half on each side, if two inches too large, *vice versa;* no matter what the amount of difference is, take one-half the amount and move the dart points that amount nearer together if too small; if too large, farther apart, changing both sides equal.

CHILD'S DRESS.

Use scale corresponding with bust measure.

Is in six pieces: Front, Back, two Sleeve Portions, one-half of Sash and one-half of Skirt.

This is drafted out upon the general plan of work.

The skirt is gathered at the top and sewed at the waist, the sash is made in a large bow in the center of the back, with long ends extending to the bottom of the dress.

Regulate the length by the use of the tape measure.

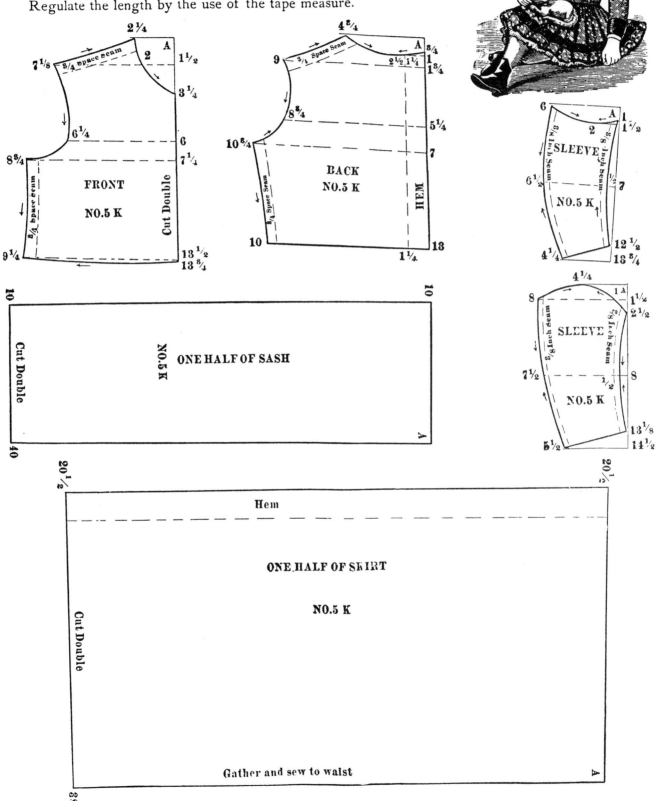

LADIES' PLAIN BASQUE.

This Basque is especially for stout forms.

Use scale corresponding with bust measure.

Is in seven pieces: Front, Back, Side Back, two under-arm Gores, and two Sleeve Portions.

This Basque is drafted upon the general plan of work. Connect the waist lines.

Regulate the length by the use of the tape measure.

If measure is over 45 inches, use a scale for length that requires only very slight change of length, or no change.

Then deduct six inches from measure and divide by 2; this gives scale for widths.

If measure was 48 deduct 6, giving 42, divide by 2; this gives 21. Use scale 21, and use each number twice on cross lines, instead of once as in all other drafts.

If measure should be an odd number, take a little loose or tight, so as to give an even number. Loose is preferable.

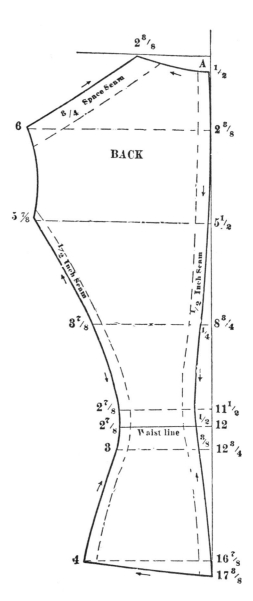

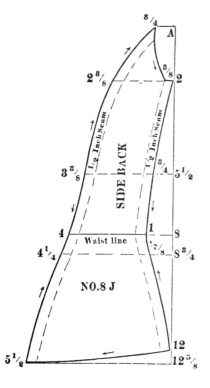

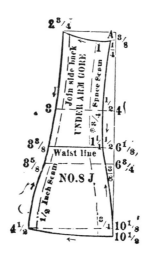

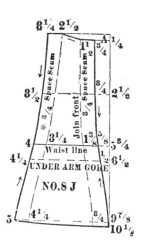

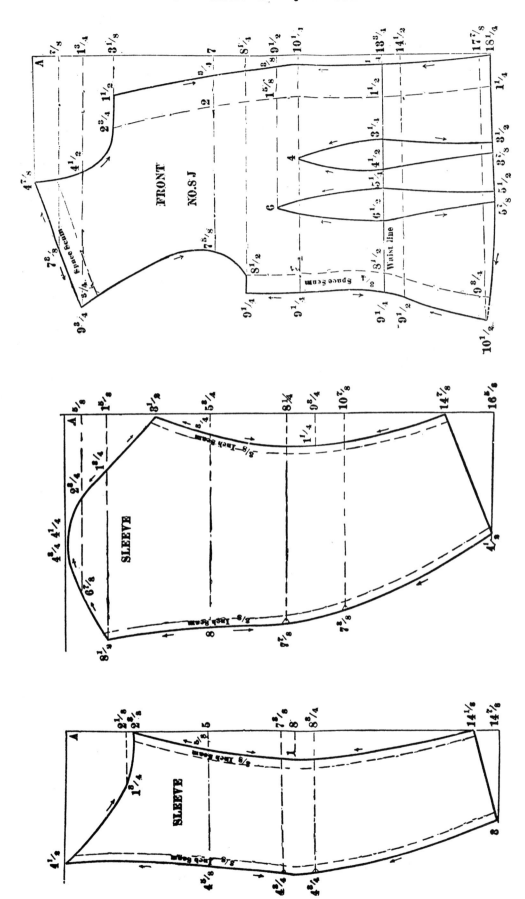

LADIES' COSTUME.

THE BASQUE

Is drafted by the scale corresponding with the bust measure.

Is in six pieces: Front, Back, Side Back, Vest Front and two Sleeve portions.

TO MAKE BASQUE

Like the figure shows, draft the front upon the general plan of work.

Trace from 2¼ on top measure line down to 11 on base line, then from 11 on base line to 2 on cross measure line and down to 1½ on cross measure line at the bottom of the basque. Cut this out, allowing enough to turn under and fasten to the Vest Front.

THE VEST FRONT

is sewed in the first dart, and extends to 4¾ on one cross measure line at the shoulder.

THE BACK

Can be cut plain, if preferred.

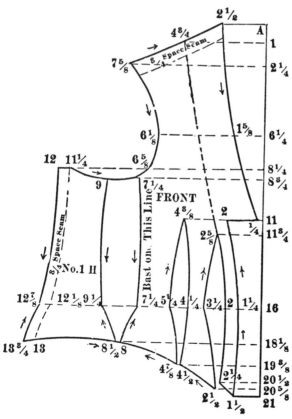

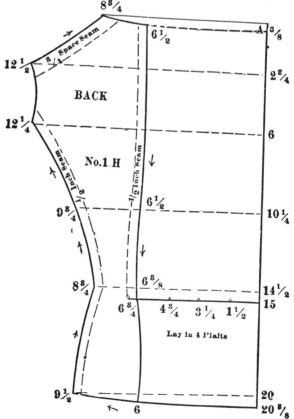

22

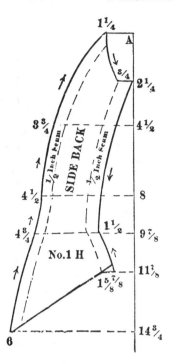

Side Back piece labels: $1\frac{1}{4}$, A, $\frac{3}{4}$, $2\frac{1}{4}$, $4\frac{1}{2}$, $3\frac{3}{4}$, $\frac{1}{2}$ Inch Seam, SIDE BACK, $\frac{1}{2}$ Inch Seam, $4\frac{1}{2}$, 8, $4\frac{3}{4}$, $1\frac{1}{2}$, $9\frac{7}{8}$, No.1 H, $11\frac{7}{8}$, $1\frac{5}{8}$, $14\frac{3}{4}$, 6

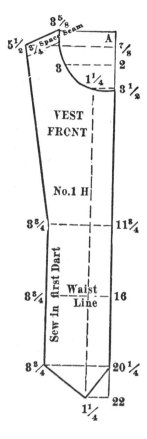

Vest Front labels: $8\frac{5}{8}$, $5\frac{1}{2}$, $\frac{5}{4}$, Space, Seam, A, $\frac{7}{8}$, 2, 3, $1\frac{1}{4}$, $3\frac{1}{2}$, VEST FRONT, No.1 H, $3\frac{3}{4}$, $11\frac{3}{4}$, Sew in first Dart, Waist Line, $8\frac{3}{4}$, 16, $8\frac{3}{4}$, $20\frac{1}{4}$, 22, $1\frac{1}{4}$

LADIES' KILT SKIRT.

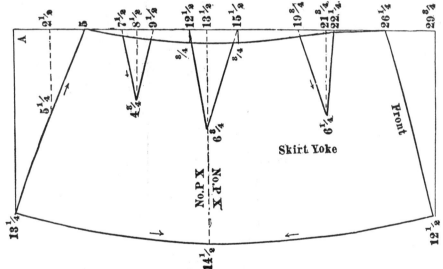

Skirt Yoke labels: A, $2\frac{1}{8}$, 5, $7\frac{7}{8}$, $8\frac{1}{2}$, $9\frac{1}{2}$, $12\frac{1}{2}$, $13\frac{1}{2}$, $15\frac{1}{8}$, $19\frac{3}{4}$, $21\frac{1}{8}$, $22\frac{1}{4}$, $26\frac{1}{4}$, $29\frac{3}{4}$, $\frac{3}{4}$, $\frac{3}{4}$, $5\frac{1}{4}$, $4\frac{3}{4}$, $6\frac{1}{4}$, $6\frac{1}{4}$, No.P X, No.P X, Skirt Yoke, Front, $13\frac{1}{4}$, $14\frac{1}{2}$, $12\frac{1}{2}$

Use scale corresponding with waist measure.

Is in two pieces: Yoke and Plaiting for skirt.

There are 36 plaits in the skirt. But 11 ½ are here given, the balance are drafted accordingly.

Press the plaits carefully and sew to the yoke.

Regulate the length by the tape measure.

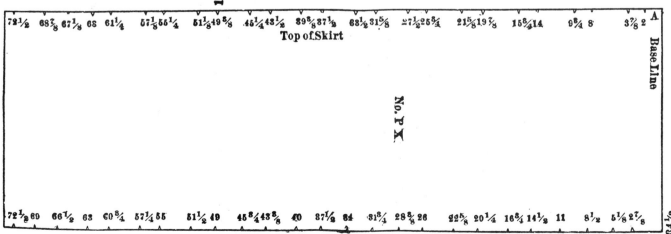

| 72½ | 68⅞ | 67⅛ | 68 | 61¼ | 57⅝ | 55¼ | 51⅛ | 49⅝ | 45¼ | 43⅛ | 39⅜ | 37⅛ | 33⅛ | 31⅝ | 27½ | 25¾ | 21⅝ | 19⅞ | 15⅝ | 14 | 9¼ | 8 | 3⅞ | 2 | A |

Top of Skirt

No.P X

Base Line

| 72⅛ | 69 | 66½ | 63 | 60¾ | 57¼ | 55 | 51½ | 49 | 45⅜ | 43⅜ | 40 | 37½ | 34 | 31¾ | 28⅜ | 26 | 22⅝ | 20¼ | 16⅝ | 14½ | 11 | 8½ | 5⅛ | 2⅞ | 34⅛ |

LADIES' COSTUME.

This is a beautiful basque, with vest front and single front dart. The drapery only of the skirt is given, as the under part of the skirt is cut plain, with a row of narrow plaiting at the bottom.

TO CUT BASQUE,

Take measure and follow instructions same as in first basque.

The vest part can be of any material desired.

The skirt is drafted by waist measure.

In making the basque, if the lining is all that is cut as far back as the under arm dart, the vest proper will have to be stitched firmly upon the lining.

The trimming on the side drapery should be a straight strip, four to six inches wide.

The sleeve may have a cuff put upon it of same material as vest and trimming on side drapery, with very pleasant effect.

The back of the basque is cut plain and no trimming used.

The collar is a straight band the width desired.

THE DRAPERY

is cut in two pieces: Back Drapery and Front Drapery.

Turn eight plaits towards the center in the back drapery as shown by the numbers on top measure line. Only one-half the drapery is given, and four plaits are shown in the part given.

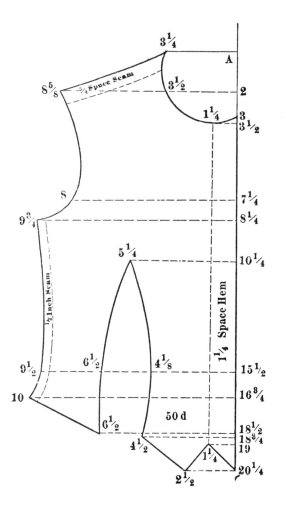

Turn the first plait by laying the notch at 20¾ on the center, the next plait by placing 14¼ on 19¾, 7¾ on 13¼, and 1 on 6½. This gives the plaits on right side. Lay plait on left side the same, and securely fasten to the band.

Lay four plaits at the side in the same manner, according to the figures given.

Turn four plaits on front drapery as shown by the figures.

Fasten the right side of the drapery with ornaments, leaving it open below the last ornament. The left side is fastened all the way down. The skirt has a plain narrow plaiting at the bottom.

24

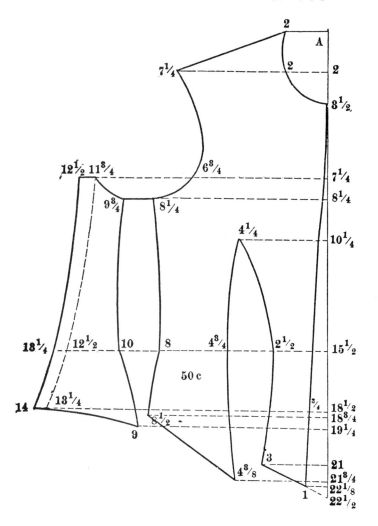

50 c

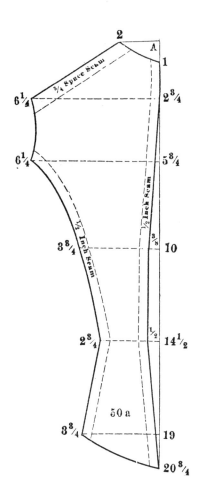

50 a

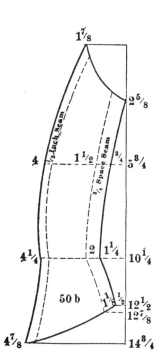

50 b

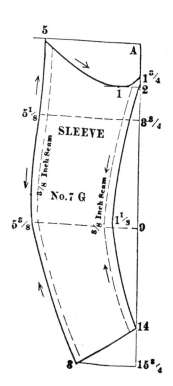

SLEEVE

No. 7 G

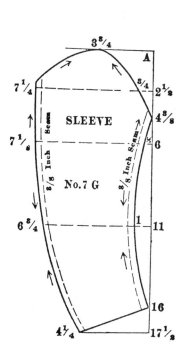

SLEEVE

No. 7 G

LADIES' COSTUME—Continued.

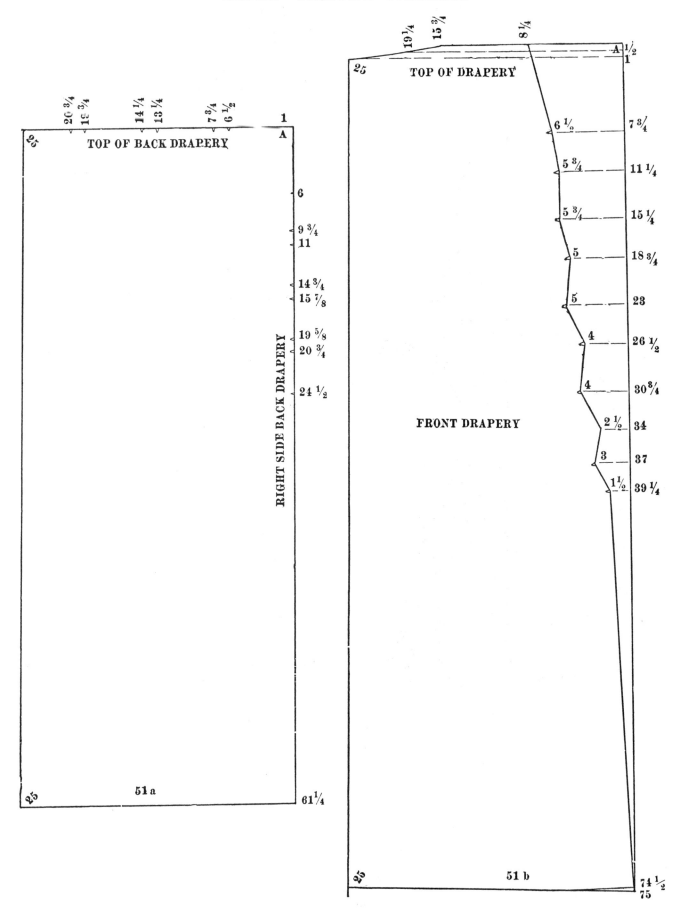

TOP OF BACK DRAPERY

20 ¾   18 ¾   14 ¼   13 ¼   7 ¾   6 ½   1

A

25

RIGHT SIDE BACK DRAPERY

6

9 ¾
11

14 ¾
15 ⅞

19 ⅝
20 ¾

24 ½

25   51 a   61¼

19 ¼   15 ¾   8 ¼   A ½
1

25   **TOP OF DRAPERY**

6 ½   7 ¾

5 ¾   11 ¼

5 ¾   15 ¼

5   18 ¾

5   23

4   26 ½

4   30 ⅜

2 ½   34

3   37

1 ½   39 ¼

FRONT DRAPERY

25   51 b   74 ½
75

LADIES' TEA GOWN.

THE PLAITING

For the front is laid in five forward turning plaits and fastened to the lining, and the upper front is blind stitched over it.

The revers of velvet may be omitted. If preferred, lace may be used, with a very pleasing effect.

THE BACK

Is laid in two double box plaits.

Care should be taken to connect waist lines.

Regulate the length by the use of the tape measure.

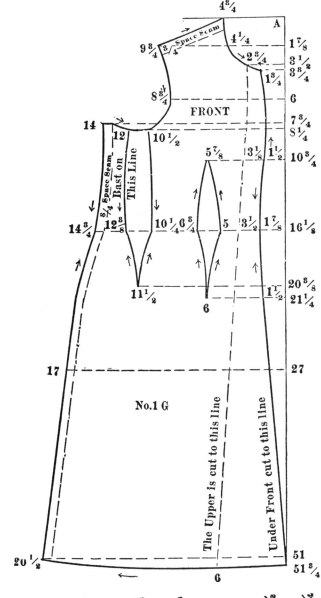

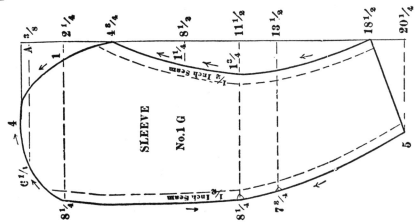

Use scale corresponding with the bust measure.

Is in seven pieces: Front, Back, Side Back, Plaiting for Front, Collar and two Sleeve portions.

The line on the front marked under front is to cut the lining out by, and the line marked upper front is to cut the goods out by, that the Tea Gown is to be made of.

27

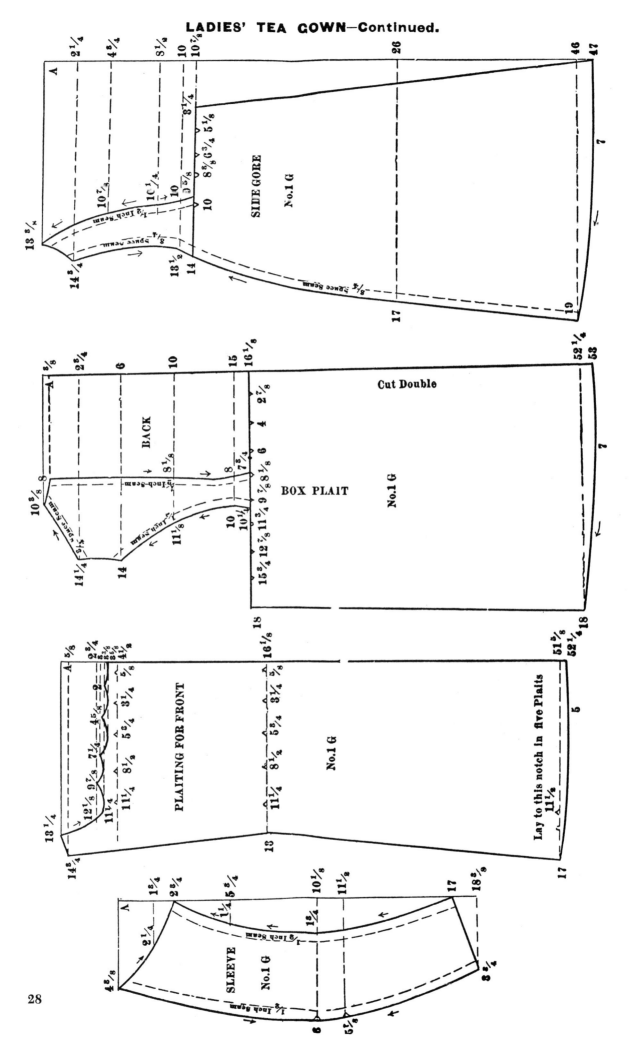

SIDE GORE
No. 1 G

BACK
Cut Double
No. 1 G
BOX PLAIT

PLAITING FOR FRONT
No. 1 G
Lay to this notch in five Plaits

SLEEVE
No. 1 G

28

Draft the back and side of Basque upon the same plan given in first basque.

DRAFT FRONT

By drawing base line at least three spaces from edge of material. Make the draft as shown in diagram.

TO GET RIGHT FRONT

Turn under the material on line $1\frac{1}{4}$ spaces from base line. Take a tracing wheel and trace the line beginning on the point at $1\frac{1}{4}$ on third cross line out to $3\frac{1}{2}$. Follow the line down to 4 on next line below. Follow this line by tracing down by points marked 4, $3\frac{1}{4}$ to $1\frac{1}{4}$ on waist line.

Turn this back and cut the goods on the tracing line outside of base line and to $1\frac{1}{4}$ waist line. This gives the right front.

THE LEFT FRONT

Is cut on the line in draft same as any other plain front.

Instead of cutting diagonal as has been given, the basque may be cut full double-breasted by running line as much farther back as desired, than is here given; then running the line down to top of first dart, and following first line of dart down to bottom of basque.

Gather the sleeve, making notches; join at elbow.

Collar is a straight band, width and length desired.

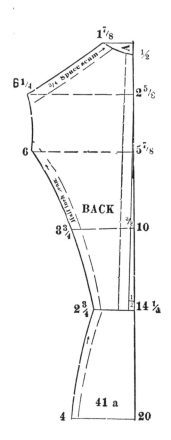

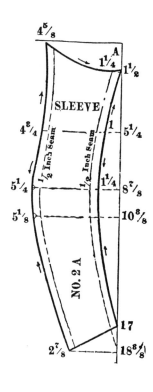

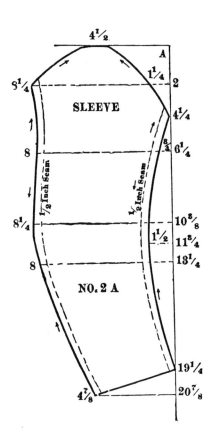

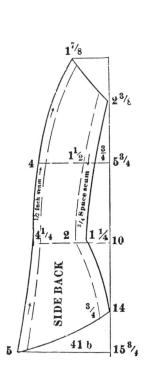

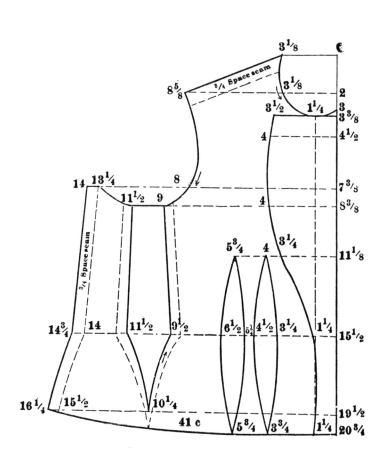

BACK AND SIDE DRAPERY.

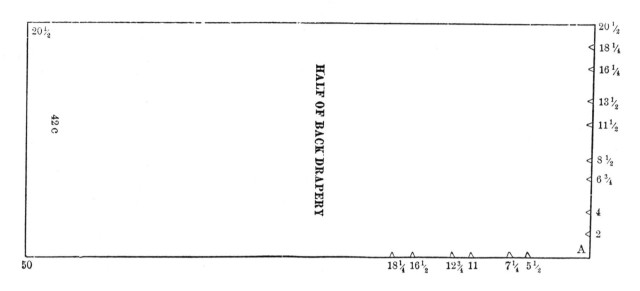

Only one-half of each of drapery is here given. Lay plaits in each piece to correspond with numbers given in draft.

Four plaits on each side of waist line of back drapery. Three at the side of back drapery.

Lay seven plaits in side drapery.

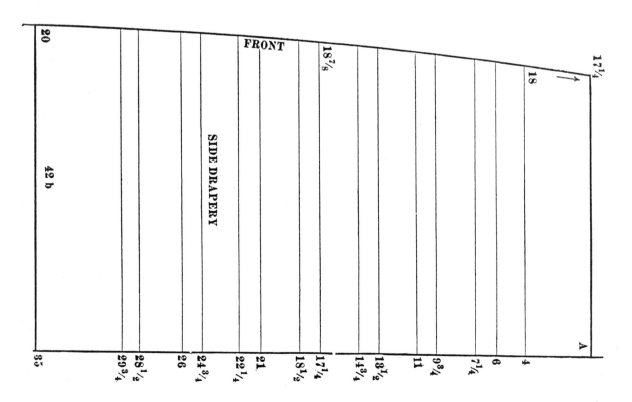

ONE-HALF FRONT DRAPERY.

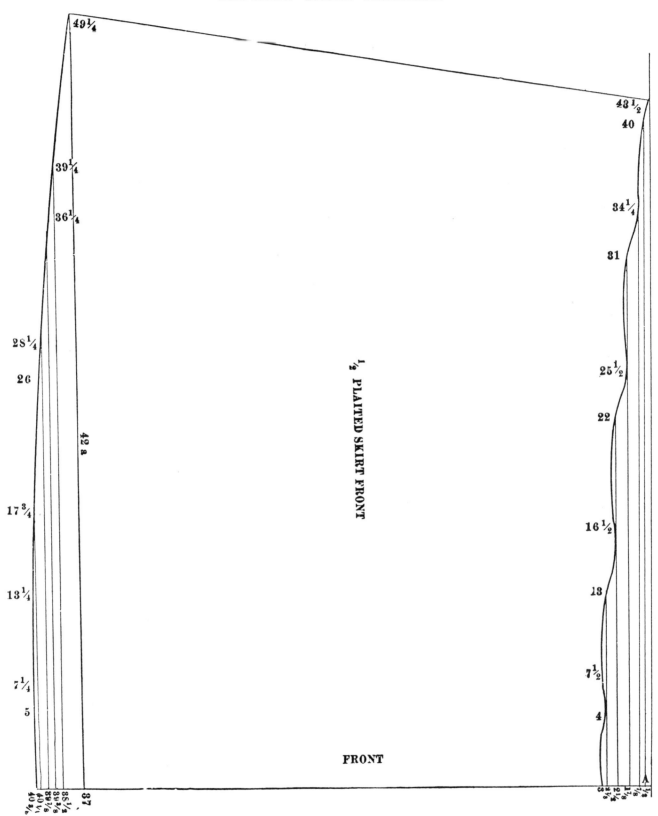

½ PLAITED SKIRT FRONT

FRONT

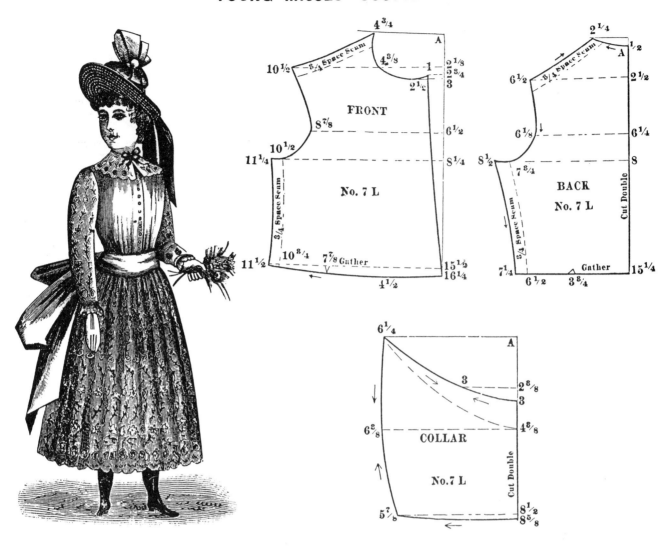

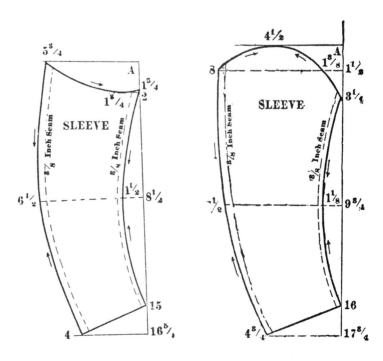

Use the scale corresponding with the bust measure.

The Waist is in five pieces: Front, Back, Collar, and two Sleeve portions.

The Belt is not given, as it is simply a straight piece of goods the length and width desired.

Gather between the notches on front and back, and sew to the belt.

The Skirt is not given, as it is made of the lace or embroidery skirting. Make it the length and width desired.

The Sash is of the same material as the waist.

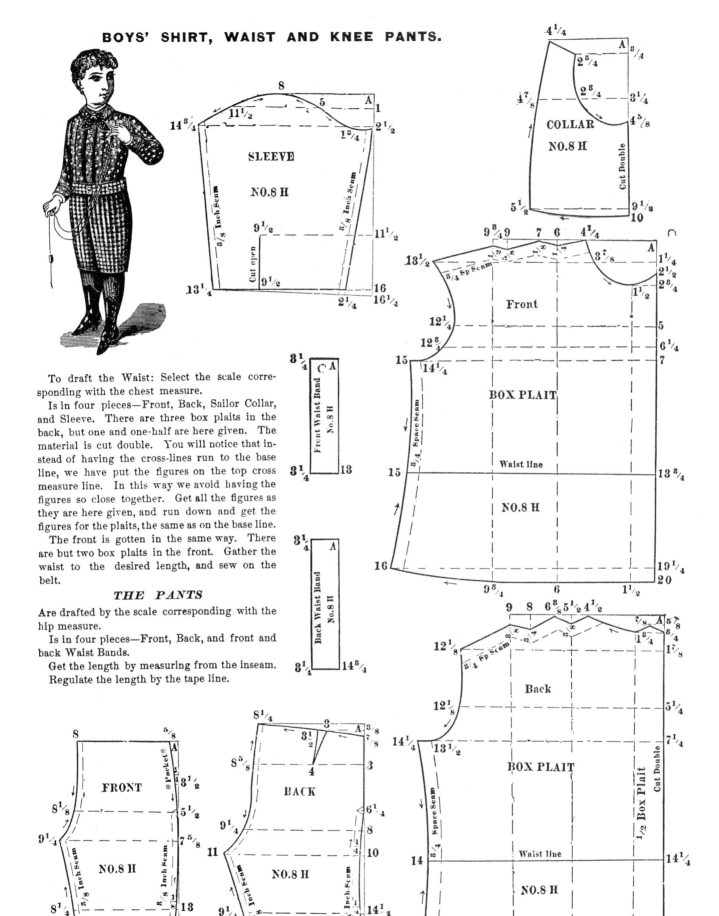

To draft the Waist: Select the scale corresponding with the chest measure.

Is in four pieces—Front, Back, Sailor Collar, and Sleeve. There are three box plaits in the back, but one and one-half are here given. The material is cut double. You will notice that instead of having the cross-lines run to the base line, we have put the figures on the top cross measure line. In this way we avoid having the figures so close together. Get all the figures as they are here given, and run down and get the figures for the plaits, the same as on the base line.

The front is gotten in the same way. There are but two box plaits in the front. Gather the waist to the desired length, and sew on the belt.

THE PANTS

Are drafted by the scale corresponding with the hip measure.

Is in four pieces—Front, Back, and front and back Waist Bands.

Get the length by measuring from the inseam. Regulate the length by the tape line.

GENTLEMEN'S DRAWERS.

Select the scale corresponding with the waist measure. It is in two pieces—one-half of drawers, and fly and waist-band combined; this is simply a facing on the outside, instead of a binding.

The measures are taken from inseam. Regulate the length by the tape measure.

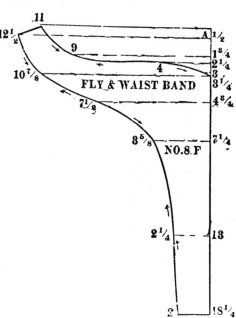

FLY & WAIST BAND

NO. 8 F

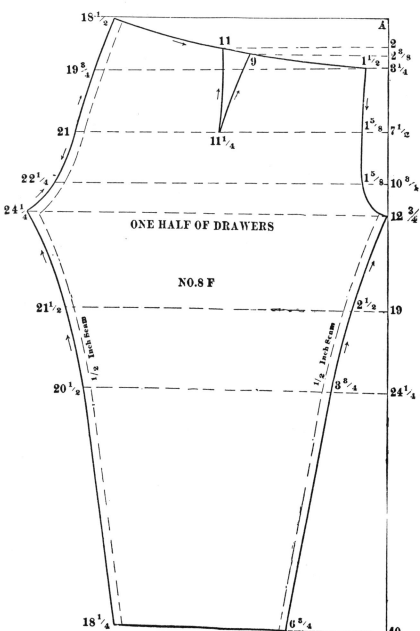

ONE HALF OF DRAWERS

NO. 8 F

½ Inch Seam

GENTLEMEN'S YOKE SHIRTS.

Use scale corresponding with the Chest measure. It is in ten pieces: Front, Back, Yoke, Neck-band, Sleeve and Sleeve Facing, Cuff Band, Facing for the Back, and Upper and Under portions for the bosom.

The front is cut out from 3⅛ on top cross measure line down to the line running from 12¼ on base line to 1⅝ on cross measure line. The extra fullness is gathered to fit the bosom.

The dotted line running from 7½ on second cross measure line to 1½ on seventh cross measure line is for the facing.

The back is to be gathered to fit the yoke.

Get length of sleeve same as any outer garment.

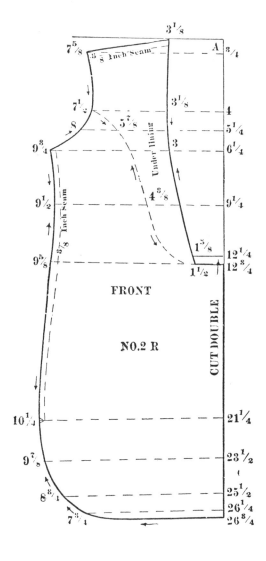

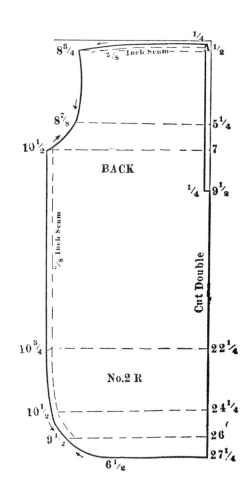

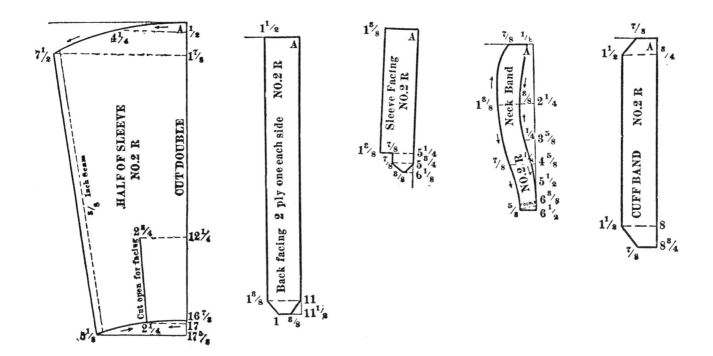

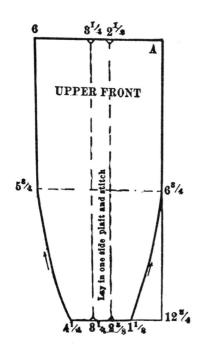

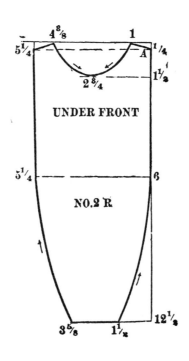

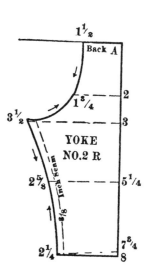

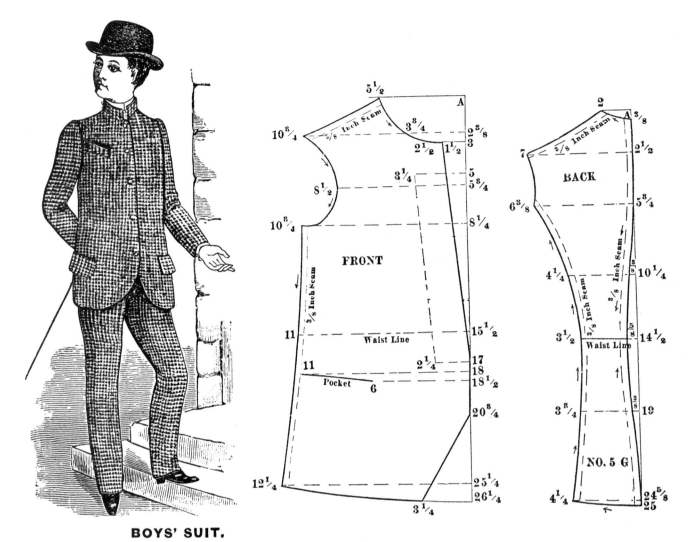

BOYS' SUIT.

The Coat and Vest are drafted by the Chest measure.

The Coat is in seven pieces: Front Back, Side Back, Collar, Pocket Lap and two Sleeve portions.

The Vest is in two pieces: Front and Back.

The Pants are drafted by the scale corresponding with the Hip measure. Is in four pieces: Front, Back, Fly and Waistband.

This is drafted upon the general plan.

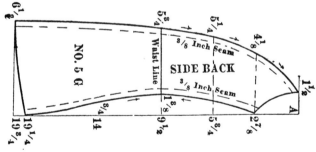

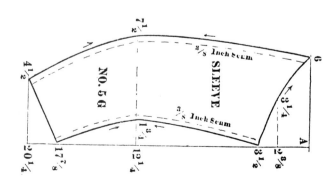

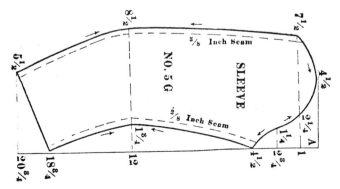

38

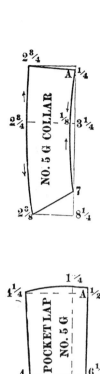

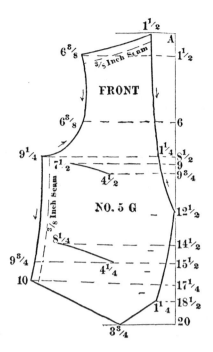

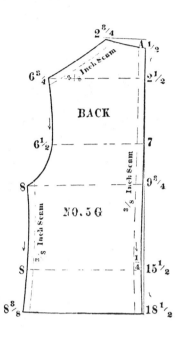

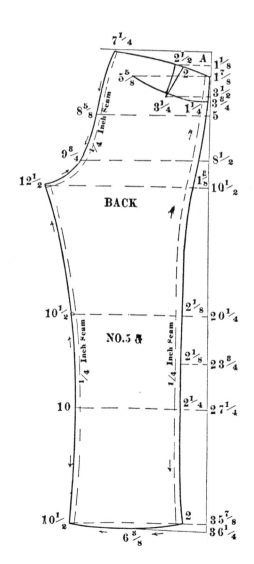

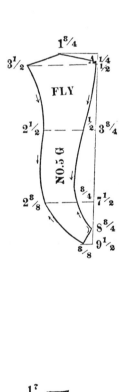

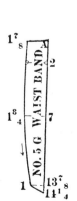

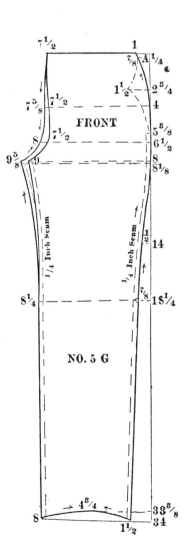

GENTLEMEN'S FOUR-BUTTON CUTAWAY.

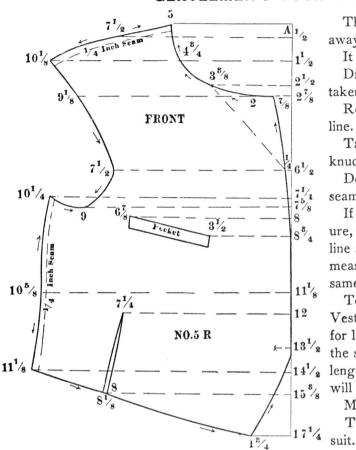

The drafts given here are for a four-button Cutaway.

It can be cut in different styles, if desired.

Draft by scale corresponding with chest measure, taken over the vest, but under the coat.

Regulate the length and size of waist by tape line.

Take measure of sleeve from center of back to knuckle-joint.

Deduct width of back piece, less one inch for seams. This gives length of sleeves.

If length of sleeve corresponds with scale measure, the length is correct; if not, change the scale line at the wrist until it corresponds with the tape measure, changing elbow line one-half the distance same direction.

To draft Vest: Take the chest measure over the Vest and use scale to correspond. Take measure for length from center of the back of the neck, over the shoulder, close to the neck, down in front the length to be worn, plus one inch for seams. This will give correct length of vest.

Make up with or without collar, as desired.

The Front can be cut either higher or lower, to suit.

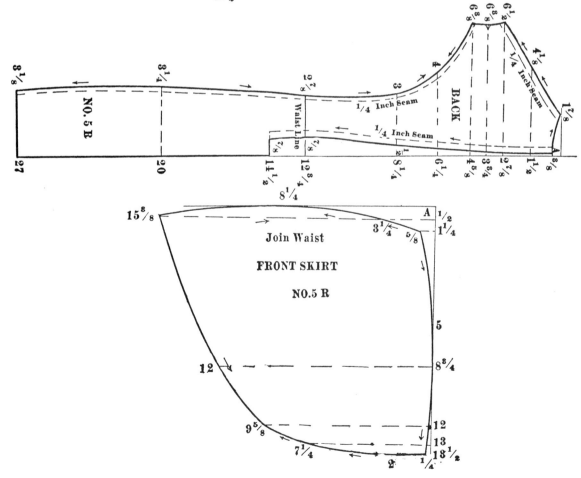

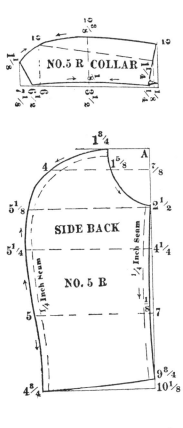

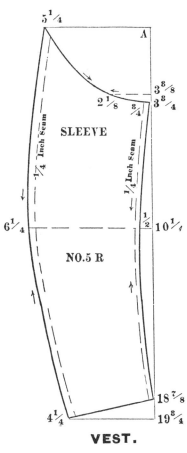

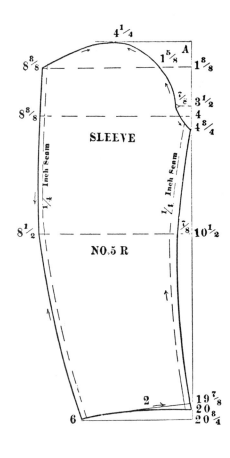

VEST.

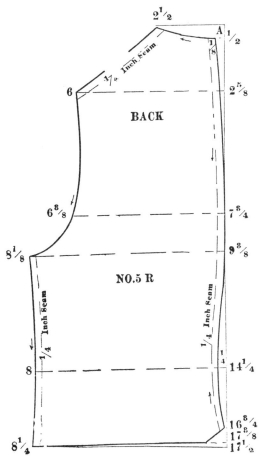

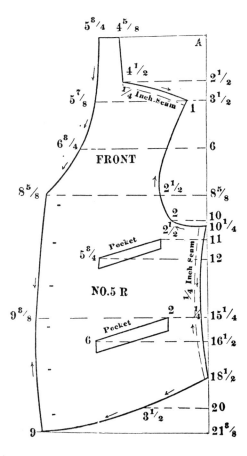

GENTLEMEN'S PANTS.

Take measure directly over hip joint. This gives number of scale to be used. Regulate size of waist and length of leg by tape measure. The size of waist, if too large or too small, is changed, one-half the amount at 8¾ on front (being cut double, this gives full amount). If change is over two inches, make part of change where front and back parts join together.

To Regulate Length.—Length is regulated by full length of garment; also by length of leg. There are two methods to measure length; one is by inseam, the other is measure from hip joint to sole of shoe. If measure is from hip joint, deduct two inches from the measure, and this gives inseam measure. Measure of pants are: Hip measure (this gives number of scale to use), Waist measure, Inseam measure, Outseam or full length. If desired in taking measures, the same result as the inseam measure can be had by measuring from the hip joint to sole of shoe, and deducting two inches. The easiest and best method to use

in testing length is to use scale corresponding with the hip measure and draft full length. Then take tape measure and measure from 11¼ on eighth cross line on back full length of inseam measure. If this measure corresponds with scale measure at 33½, the length is correct. If it does not correspond, raise or lower 33½ to tape measure. Change 33¾ same. Change point at 20¼ half the distance. Raise the lower 18½, 31 and 31⅝ on front the same distance as the corresponding figures on back were changed. Another method is to measure from 2½ base line of back to full length of garment, change scale measure to correspond, changing knee line half the distance. When full length is measured, measure back from length at bottom full length of inseam, changing point at 11¼ to tape measure. Change 9¾ same distance that you change 11¼. Change corresponding lines on front the same distance.

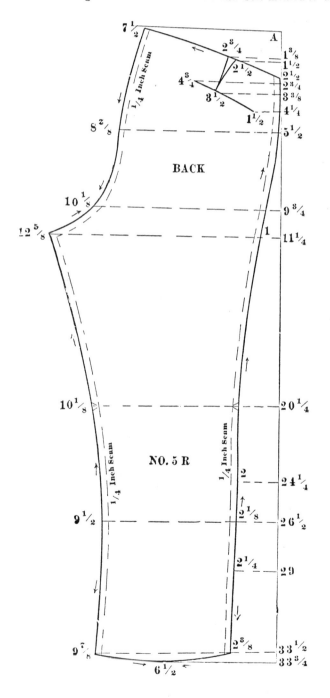

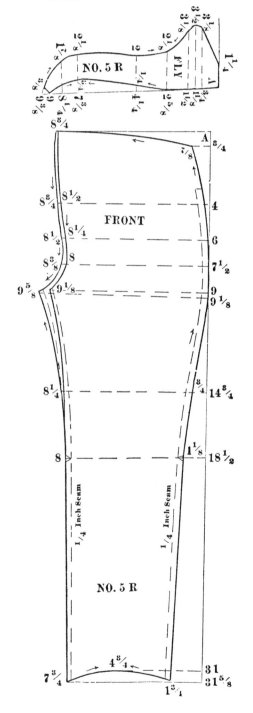

42

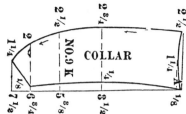

To draft the coat, take the measures moderately tight over the vest.

This is a sack coat. It is in five pieces: Front, Back, Collar and two Sleeve portions. This is drafted as all others.

The vest is also drafted by the chest measure; use the corresponding scale. It consists of Front, Back and Strap.

Regulate the length by the tape measure.

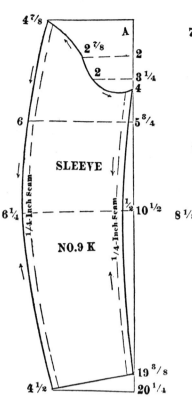

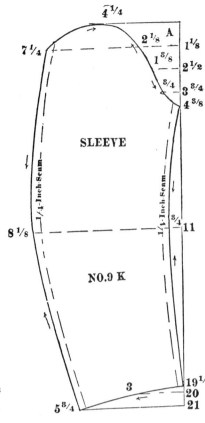

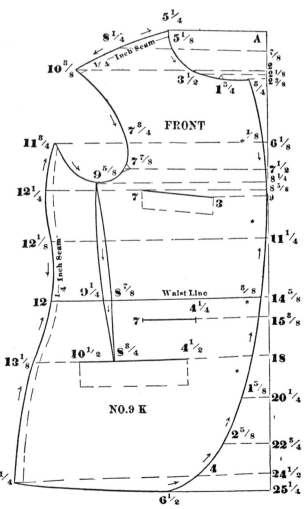

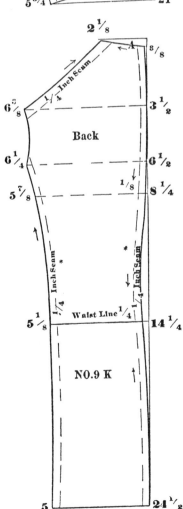

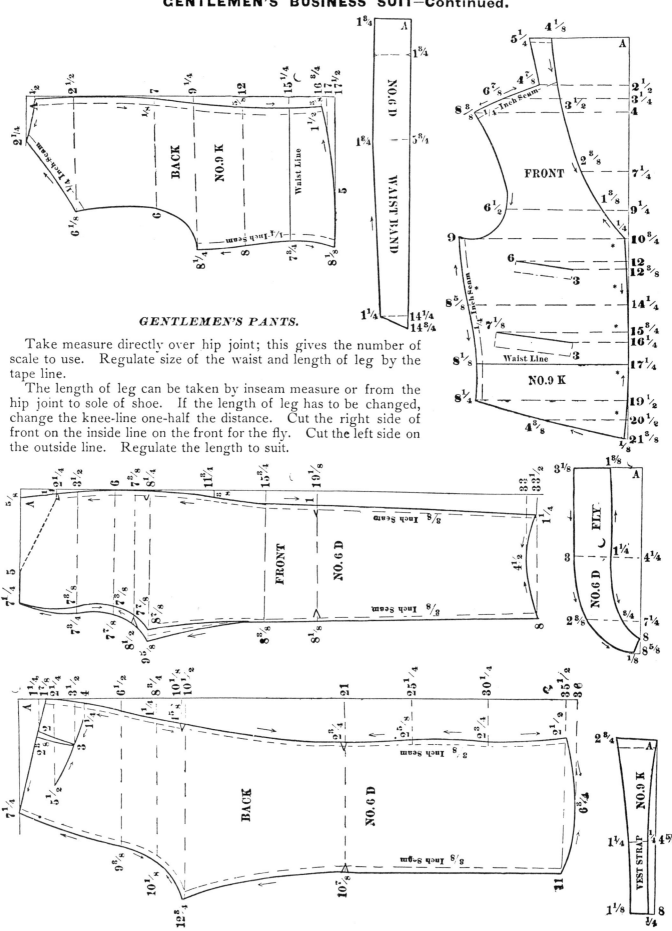

GENTLEMEN'S PANTS.

Take measure directly over hip joint; this gives the number of scale to use. Regulate size of the waist and length of leg by the tape line.

The length of leg can be taken by inseam measure or from the hip joint to sole of shoe. If the length of leg has to be changed, change the knee-line one-half the distance. Cut the right side of front on the inside line on the front for the fly. Cut the left side on the outside line. Regulate the length to suit.

CHILD'S COSTUME.

Select the scale corresponding with the bust measure.

This garment is in seven pieces: Front and Front Yoke. Back and Back Yoke, Cuff and two Sleeve portions. This is a beautiful costume and is easily made. Lay the plaits at the waist and bottom of skirt according to notches. Gather the top and sew to the Yoke: make a plain under-waist and tack the plaits to it at the waist, allowing the upper portions to fall loosely below the waist.

The sash is simply a straight piece of goods same as the dress.

The length and width desired: Regulate the length by the tape measure.

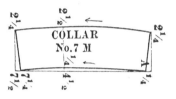

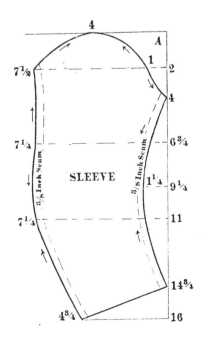

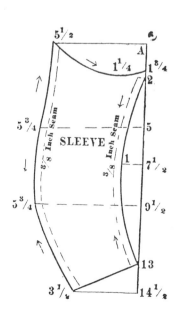

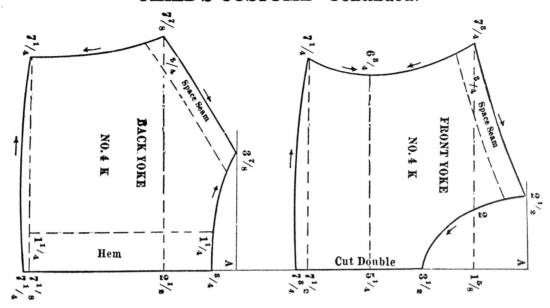

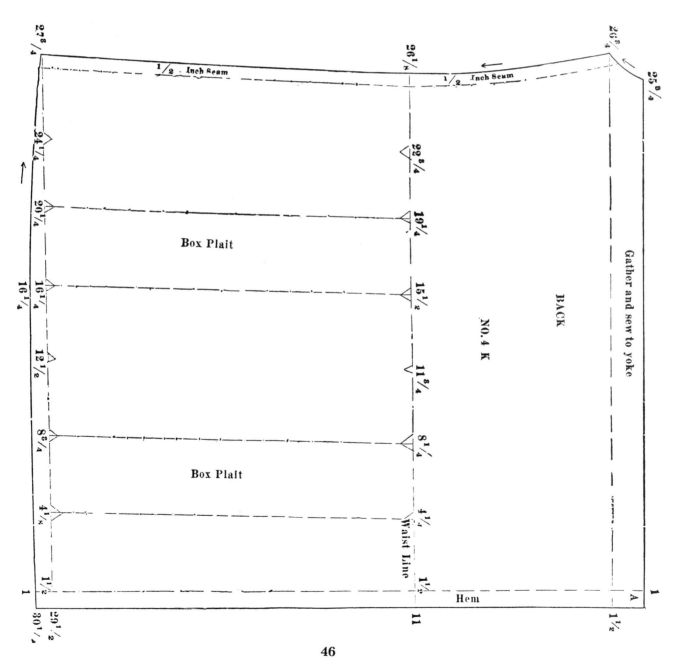

CHILD'S COSTUME—Continued.

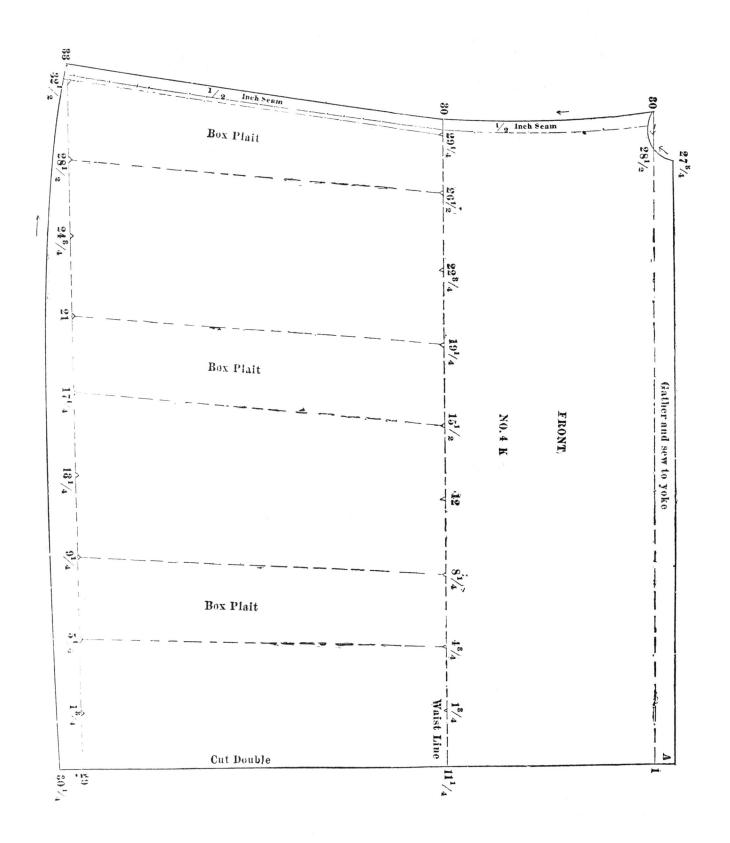

LADIES' HOUSE DRESS.

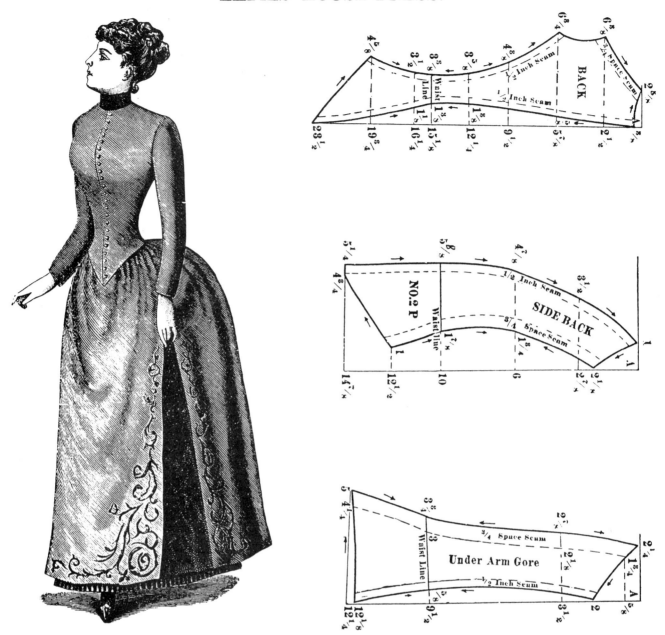

Ascertain the bust measure and use the corresponding scale to draft the Basque.

It consists of seven pieces, as follows: Front, Back, Side Back, Under Arm Gore, Collar and two Sleeve portions.

This Basque is drafted out the same as any other but the effect is different. This gives a very narrow back and rounding side back.

Cut the front darts open in the center of dart and baste on the lines given. (See diagram.)

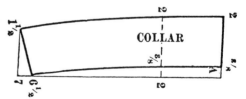

The front of Basque may be trimmed with embroidery or braiding to correspond with drapery if desired.

The skirt and drapery is drafted by the scale corresponding with the waist measure; lay pleats according to the notches.

Regulate the length by the tape measure.

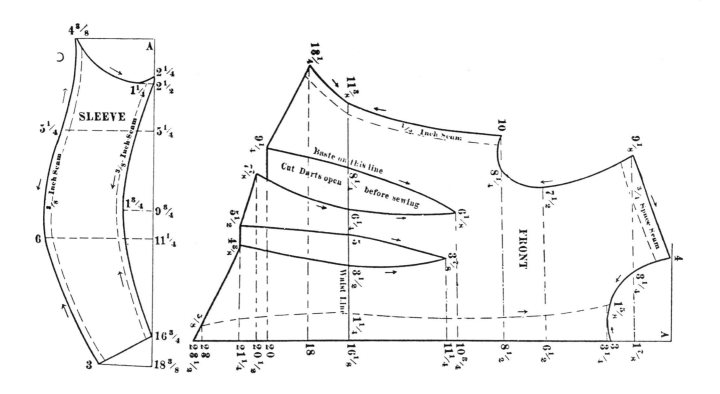

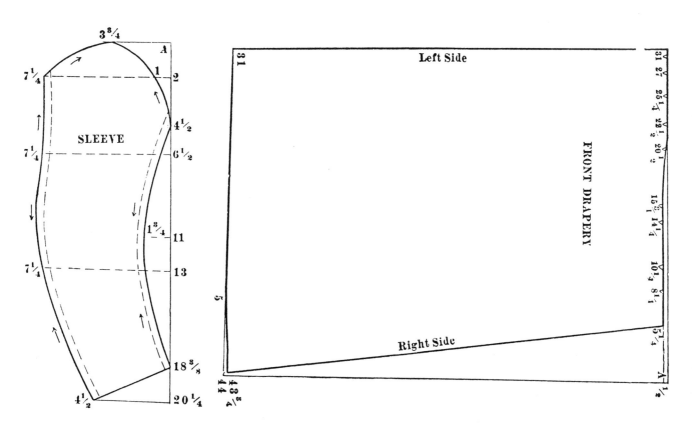

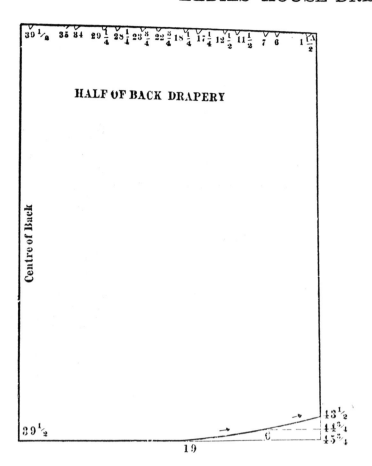

HALF OF BACK DRAPERY

Centre of Back

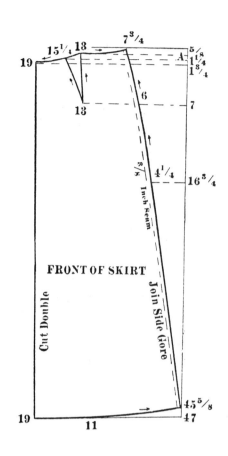

FRONT OF SKIRT

Cut Double

Join Side Gore

Inch Seam

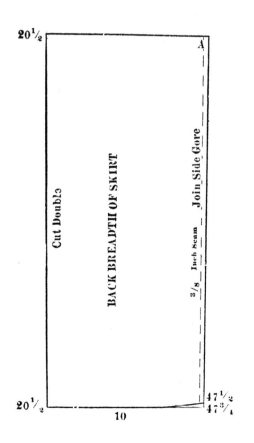

BACK BREADTH OF SKIRT

Cut Double

Join Side Gore

3/8 Inch Seam

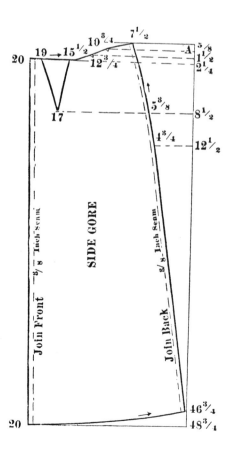

SIDE GORE

Join Front

Join Back

3/8 Inch Seam

3/8 Inch Seam

Use scale corresponding with the bust measure.

It is in eight pieces: Front, Back, the V for the front, Collar, and front of Reverse, one-half of Skirt and two Sleeve portions.

This is very suitable for a school dress.

THE SKIRT

Is shirred and sewed to the waist.

Regulate the length by the tape measure.

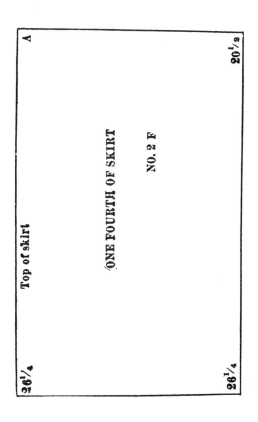

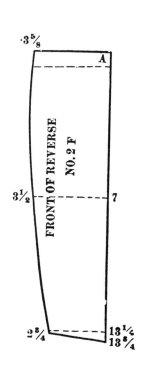

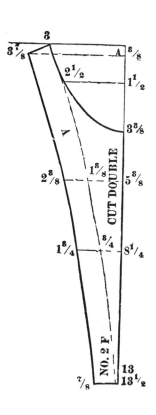

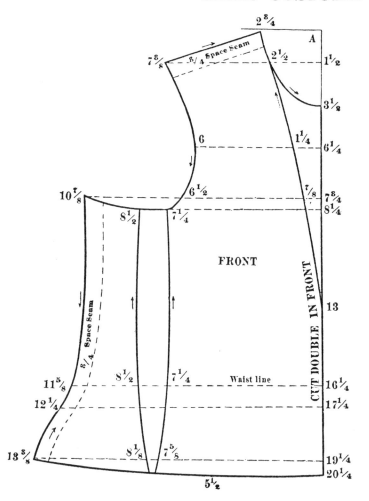

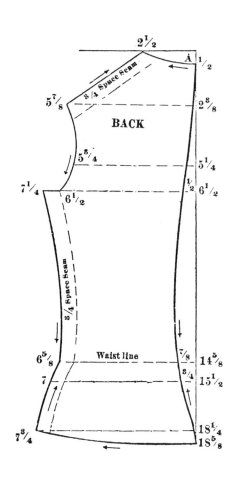

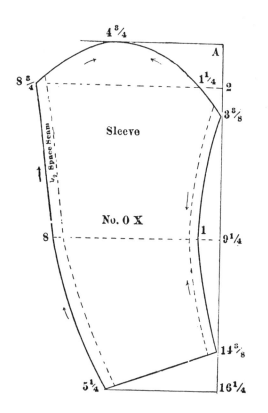

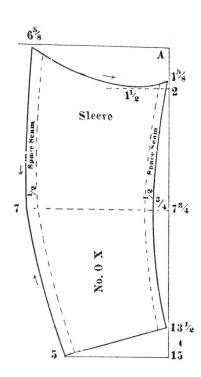

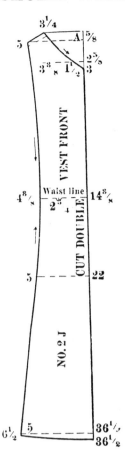

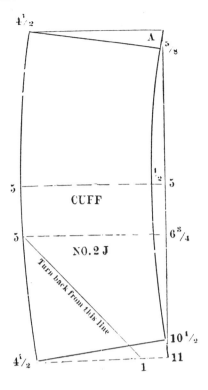

Use the scale corresponding with the Bust measure to draft the entire garment which consists of nine pieces, Front, Back, Side Back, Vest, Collar, Cuff, Hood and two Sleeve portions.

Lay the pleats in the back to form two single Box pleats.

Turn the front back on the dotted line, extending from 4½ at the neck down to 4½ at the bottom.

Sew the Vest in.

Close it on left side with hooks and eyes.

Face the Hood with any suitable material.

Regulate the length by the tape measure.

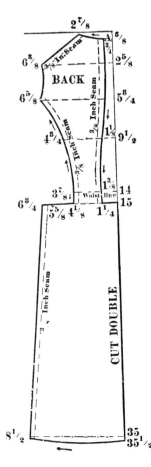

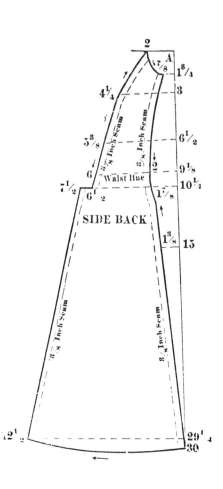

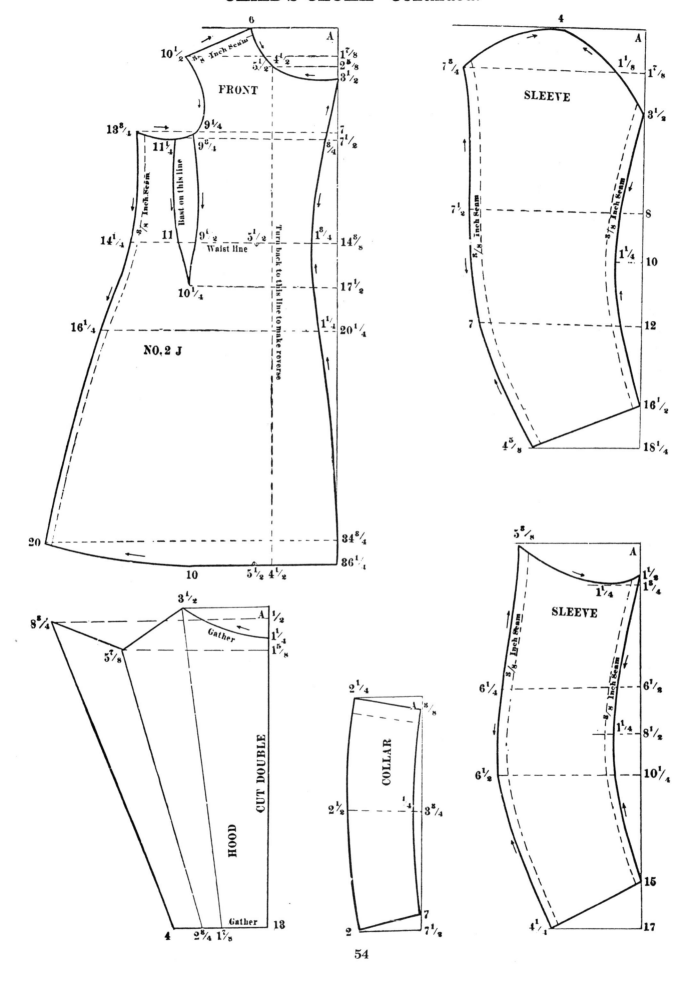

LADIES' COSTUME.

TO DRAFT THE BASQUE

Use scale corresponding with bust measure.

Is in six pieces: Front, Back, Side Back, Collar, and two Sleeve portions.

Care should be taken to connect waist lines.

THE DRAPERY.

Use scale corresponding with waist measure.

Is in two pieces: Front and Back.

The right side of the front drapery is laid in four upward turning plaits, while the left side is laid in four backward-turning plaits.

THE BACK DRAPERY.

The left side is laid in a double box plait.

The right side is laid in seven backward-turning plaits. They are all marked on the draft.

The space between 37¾ and 51½ on base line, is a loop that falls underneath the drapery. Bring 1¼ on cross measure line running from 37¾ on base line and 12¾ on cross measure line running from 51½ on base line, together at the center of the back.

This forms a lovely drapery without any looping whatever.

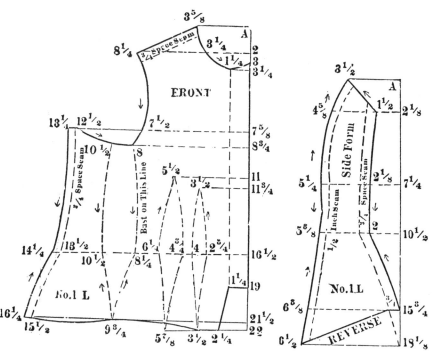

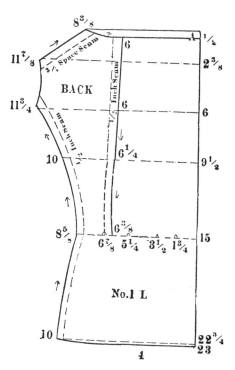

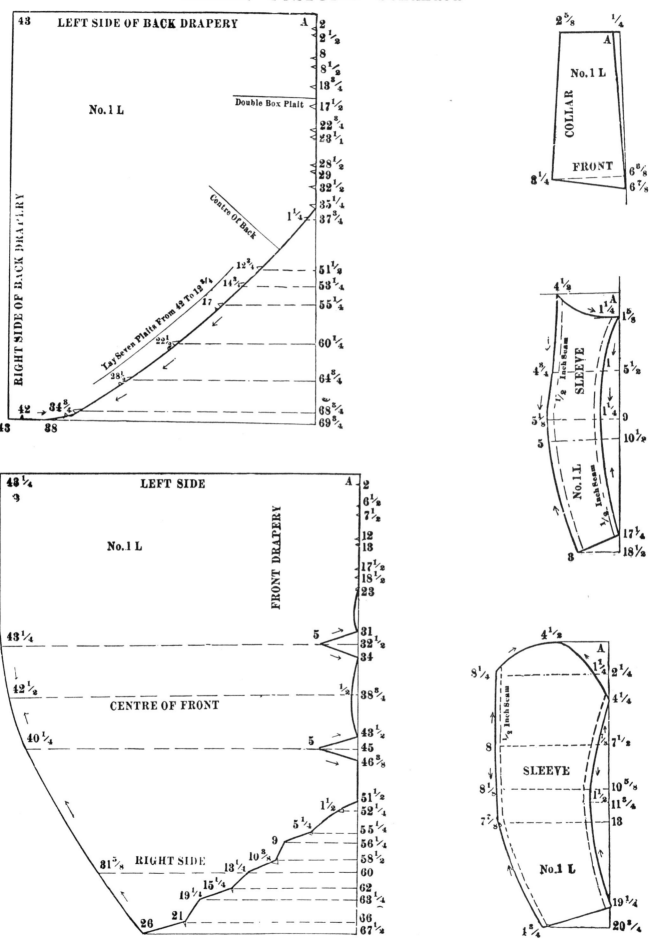

CHILD'S APRON.

Use the scale corresponding with the bust measure. Is in four pieces—front, back side piece and band.

Join back and side piece at the shoulders: sew in the front, and face all around. Any style of trimming may be used. Regulate the length by the tape measure.

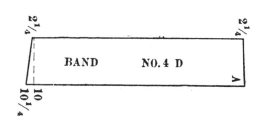

BAND   NO. 4 D

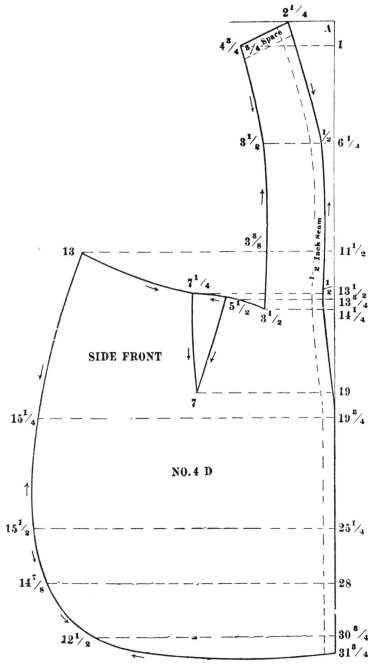

SIDE FRONT

NO. 4 D

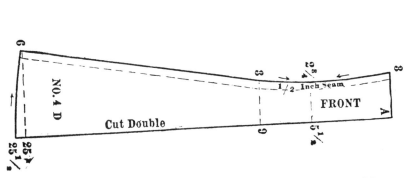

NO. 4 D

FRONT

Cut Double

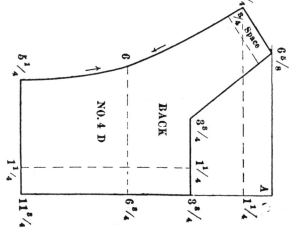

NO. 4 D   BACK

MISSES' STREET COSTUME.

TO DRAFT
THE WAIST

Use scale corresponding with the bust measure.

Is in three pieces; Front, Back and Side Back.

Is drafted upon the general plan of the work.

THE JACKET

Is drafted by scale corresponding with the bust measure.

Is in five pieces; Front, Back, Side Back and two Sleeve portions.

It has a lap on each side of the side back turning toward the center of back, and finished with three buttons on each side.

THE SKIRT

Is drafted out by the scale corresponding with the waist measure.

Only one-half is here given.

Is laid in Single Box Plaits as shown on the figure.

Can be made of any material.

THE SASH

Is of ribbon, or of the same material as the suit.

Regulate the length by the use of the tape measure.

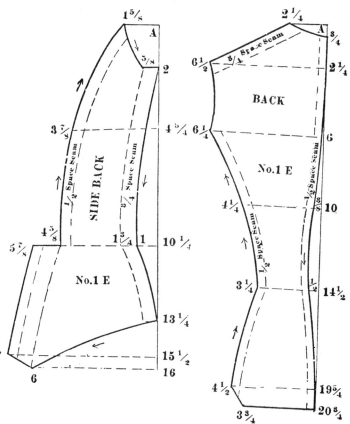

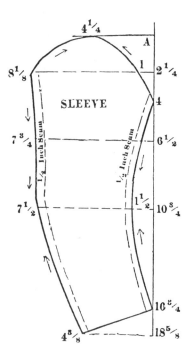

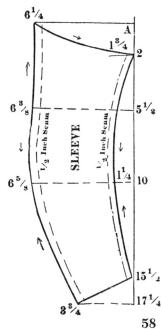

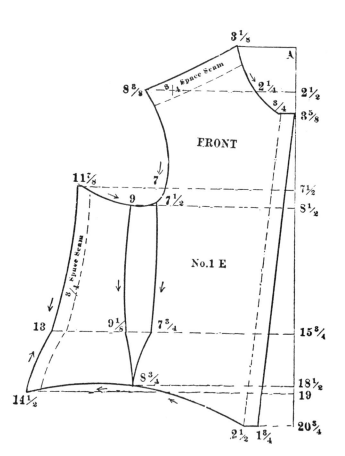

BOX PLAITED SKIRT.   LADIES' OPEN DRAWERS.

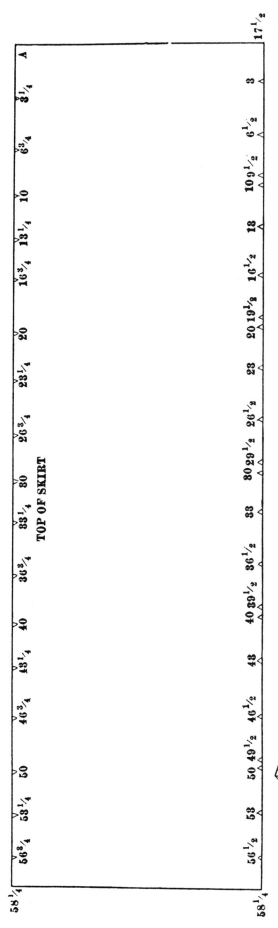

Use Scale corresponding with waist measure.

Only one-half are given.

The band can be made any width desired.

The length can be regulated by the tape measure.

Allow for the tucks.

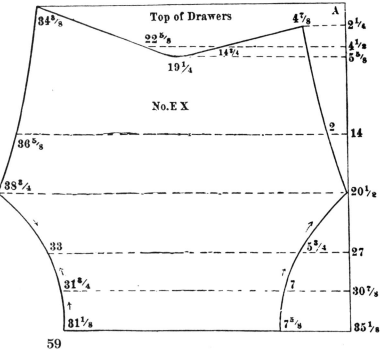

59

LADIES' WRAPPER WITH A WATTEAU.

Use scale corresponding with the bust measure.

Is in nine pieces: Front and Shirring for Front, Back, Side Back, and the Watteau, Collar and two Sleeve portions and Puff for the Sleeve.

This garment is drafted upon the general plan of work.

The shirring for the front is turned down from 1⅝ on base line to 21¼ on the cross measure line for facing. This is shirred twice and sewed to the front on the lines marked for shirring.

THE BACK.

The Watteau pleat can be omitted if preferred, when used sew it in the center of the back, down to 23 on the base line. The balance is joined together to form the fullness in the skirt.

THE SLEEVE.

The puff is gathered at the bottom and joins to the curved

ines on the sleeve marked for the puff. Sew the puff on and turn it up to the top of the sleeve; gather it at the top, and connect the notches on the puff with the notches on the sleeve, and sew them in the arm's eye

together, from the curved line where the puff is attached, down to the hand is the cuff and can be of the same material as the yoke and collar.

The length is obtained by the use of the tape measure.

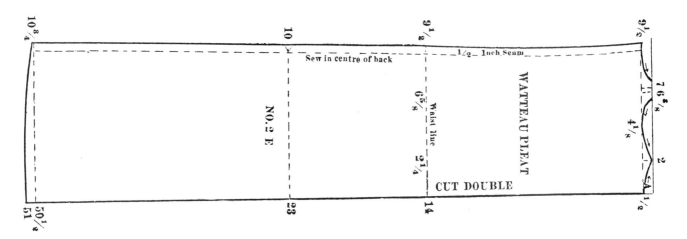

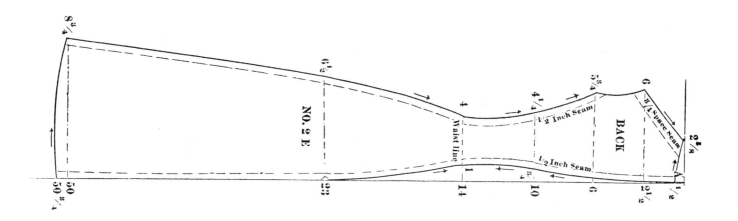

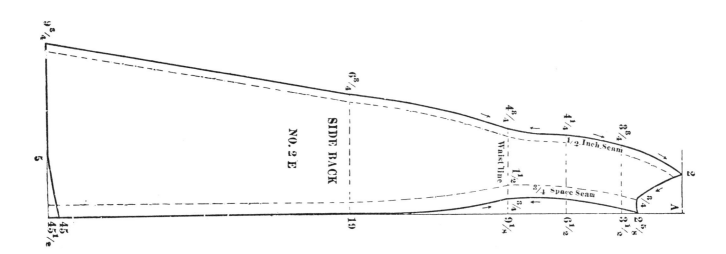

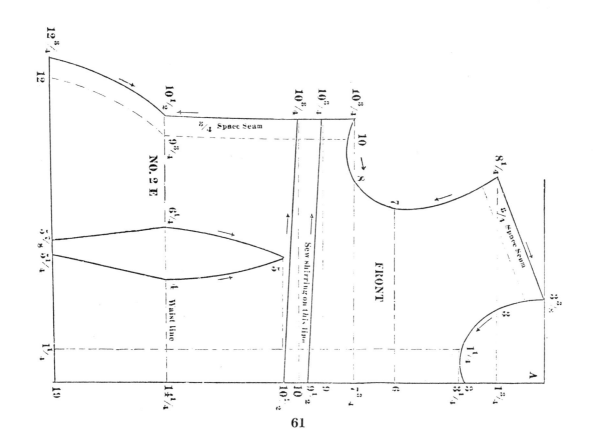

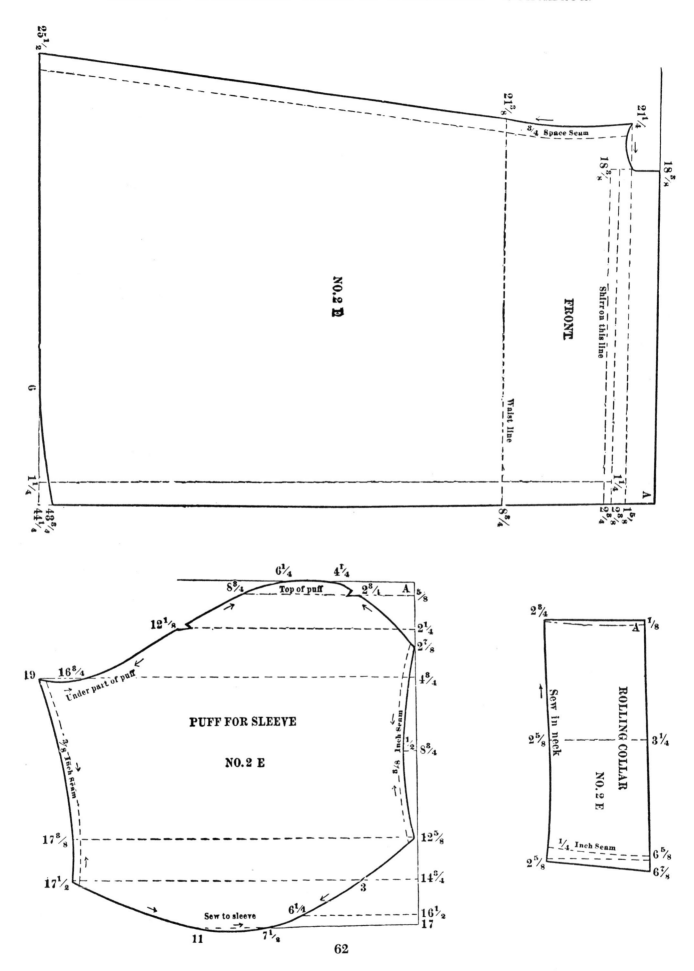

PUFF FOR SLEEVE

NO. 2 E

ROLLING COLLAR

NO. 2 E

LADIES' YOKE.

Use scale corresponding with the bust measure.

Is in two pieces: Front and Back.

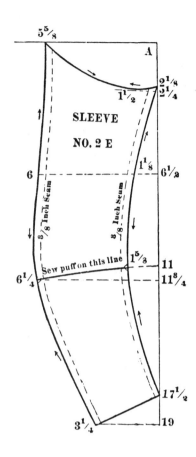

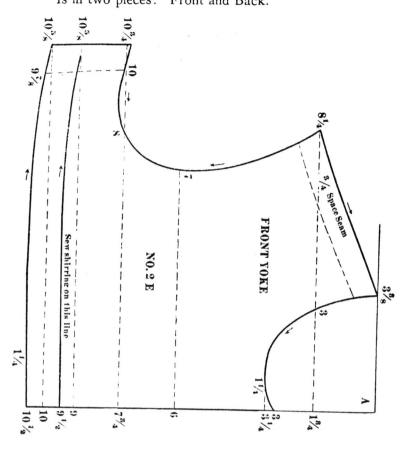

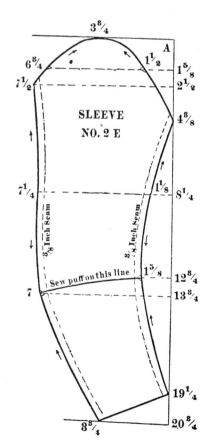

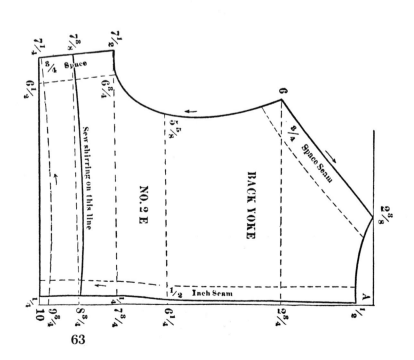

LADIES' NIGHT GOWN.

Use the scale corresponding with the bust measure to draft the entire garment. It is in four pieces—front and front yoke, back and collar. This is a Mother Hubbard front and plain back. Use any plain sleeve given in this issue. Regulate the length by the use of the tape measure.

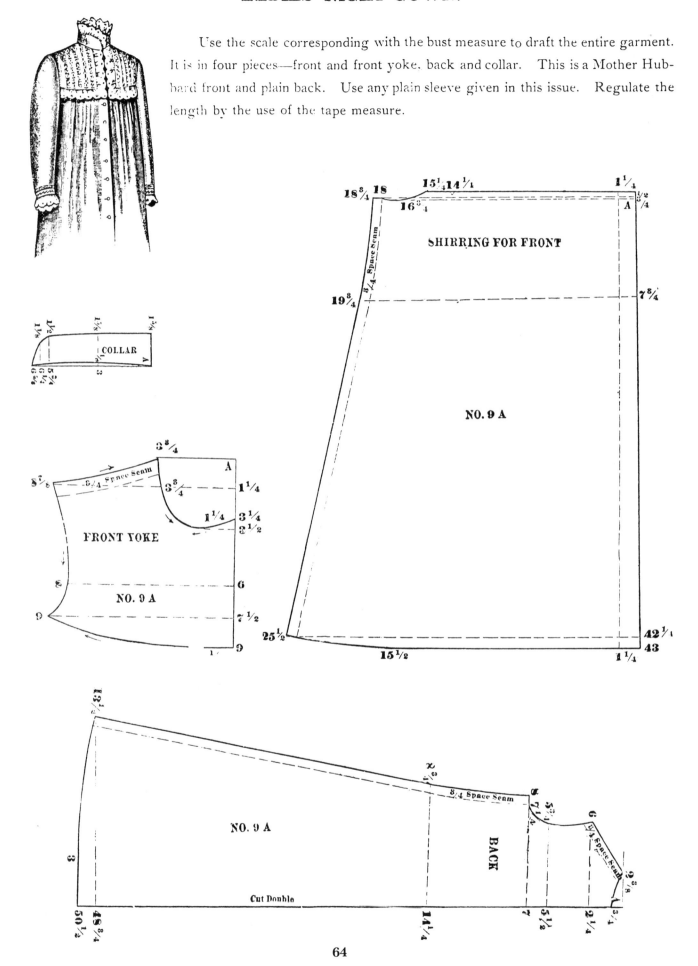

LITTLE GIRLS' DRESS.

Use scale corresponding with the bust measure.

Is in six pieces: Right and Left Front, Back Collar and two Sleeve portions.

The Sash is of Ribbon.

THE SKIRT

Is a straight piece of goods or embroidery cut the desired length and width.

The length can be obtained by the tape measure.

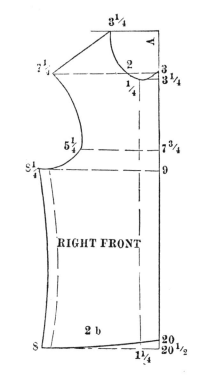

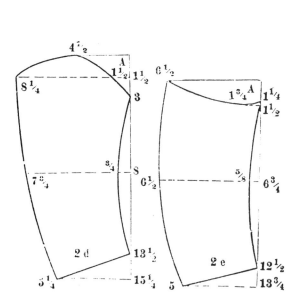

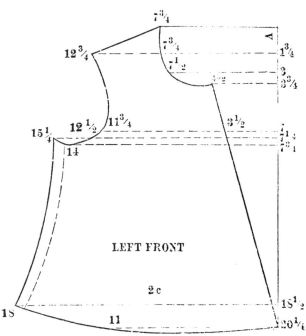

65

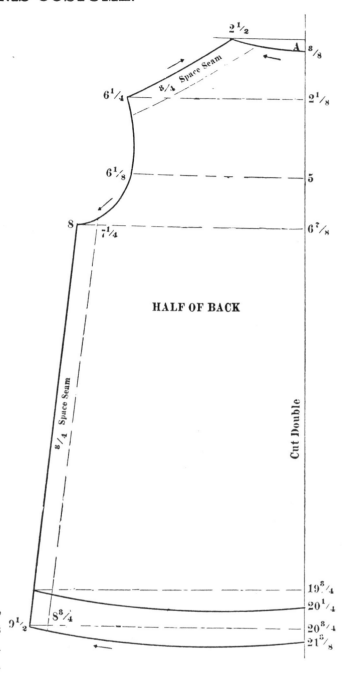

HALF OF BACK

TO DRAFT WAIST.

Use scale corresponding with the bust measure.

It consists of six pieces: Front, Back, Collar, Pocket, Cuff and Sleeve. The front is tucked as marked on diagram, the buttons are sewed underneath, and the button holes are made on the under side. The lacing in front may be omitted if preferred.

The waist is hemmed at the bottom, and insert elastic in the hem, or, if preferred, gathered and sewed to belt.

THE SKIRT.

Use scale corresponding with the waist measure.

It is in four pieces: Belt, Yoke, Sash and one-half of Kilt Skirt. The sash can be cut double if preferred. Tie around the waist and make a large knot and long ends at the side. Gather the ends of sash and finish with a tassel.

Regulate length of skirt by the tape mersure.

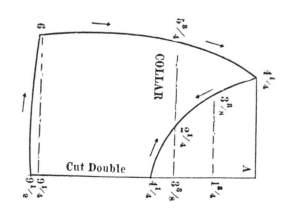

COLLAR

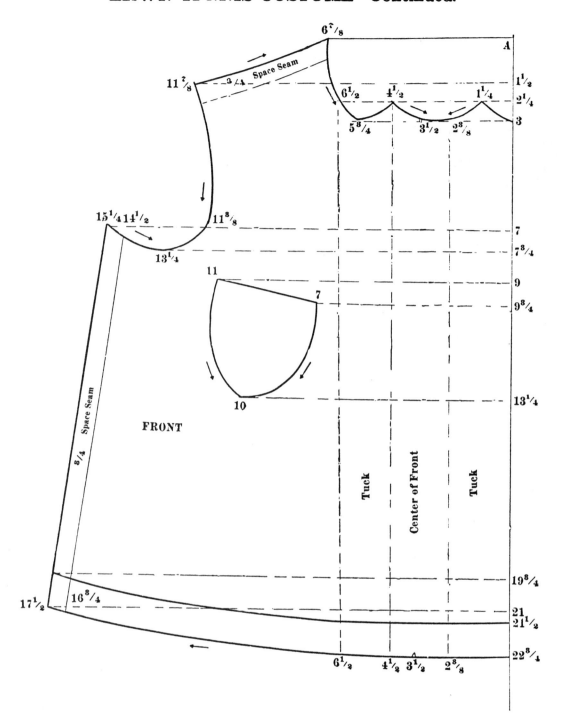

FRONT

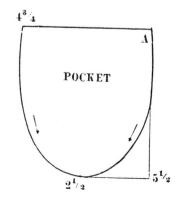

POCKET

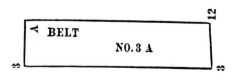

BELT

NO. 3 A

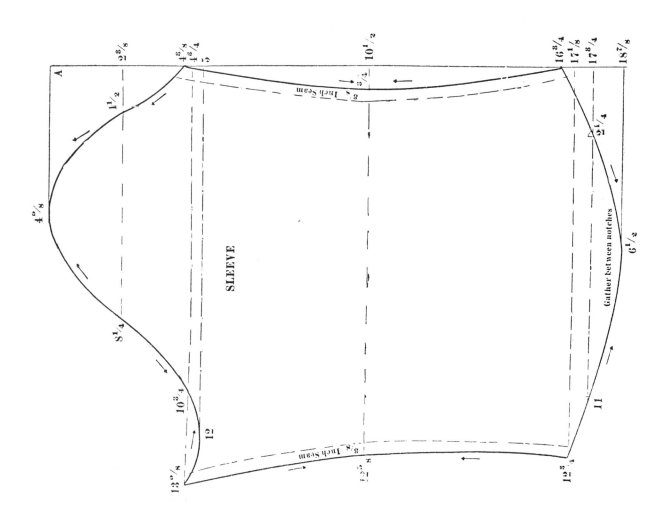

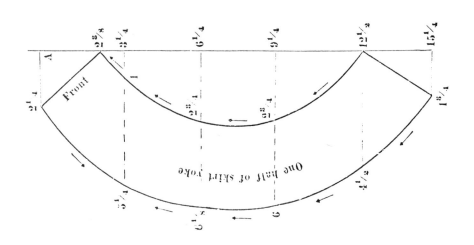

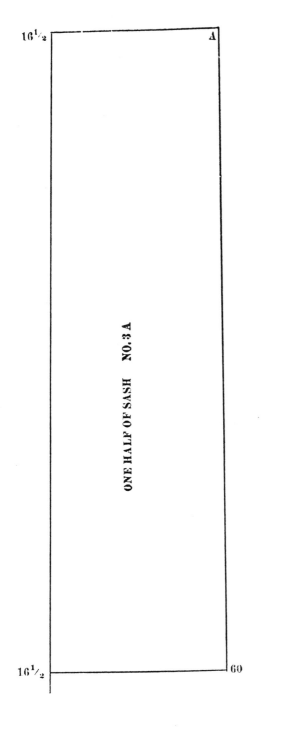

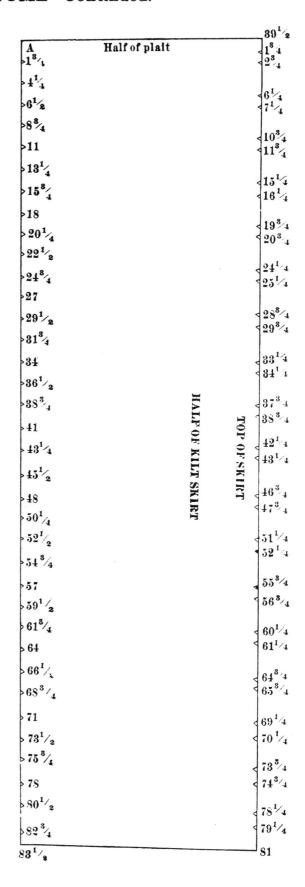

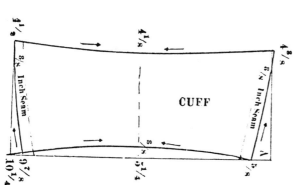

LADIES' POLONAISE.

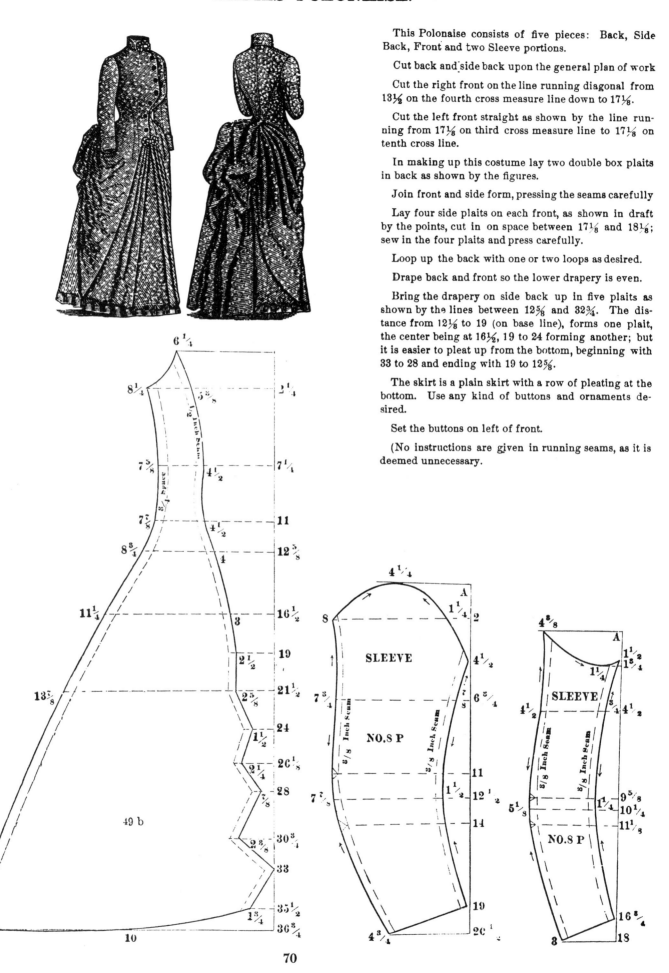

This Polonaise consists of five pieces: Back, Side Back, Front and two Sleeve portions.

Cut back and side back upon the general plan of work

Cut the right front on the line running diagonal from 13½ on the fourth cross measure line down to 17⅛.

Cut the left front straight as shown by the line running from 17⅛ on third cross measure line to 17⅛ on tenth cross line.

In making up this costume lay two double box plaits in back as shown by the figures.

Join front and side form, pressing the seams carefully

Lay four side plaits on each front, as shown in draft by the points, cut in on space between 17⅛ and 18⅛; sew in the four plaits and press carefully.

Loop up the back with one or two loops as desired.

Drape back and front so the lower drapery is even.

Bring the drapery on side back up in five plaits as shown by the lines between 12⅝ and 32¾. The distance from 12⅛ to 19 (on base line), forms one plait, the center being at 16½, 19 to 24 forming another; but it is easier to pleat up from the bottom, beginning with 33 to 28 and ending with 19 to 12⅝.

The skirt is a plain skirt with a row of pleating at the bottom. Use any kind of buttons and ornaments desired.

Set the buttons on left of front.

(No instructions are given in running seams, as it is deemed unnecessary.)

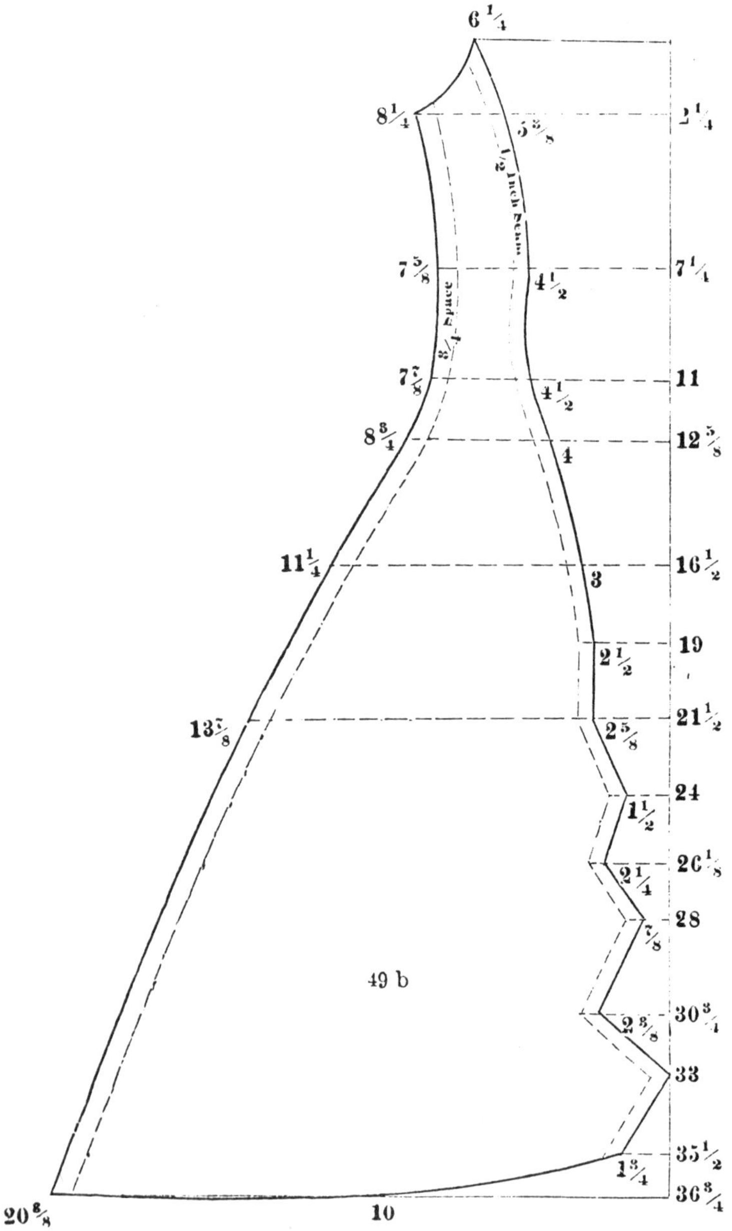

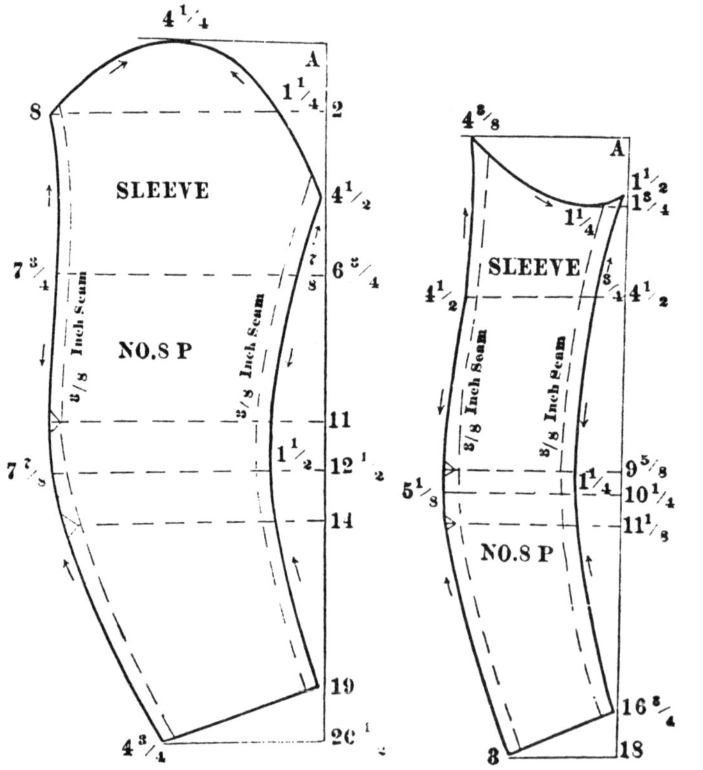

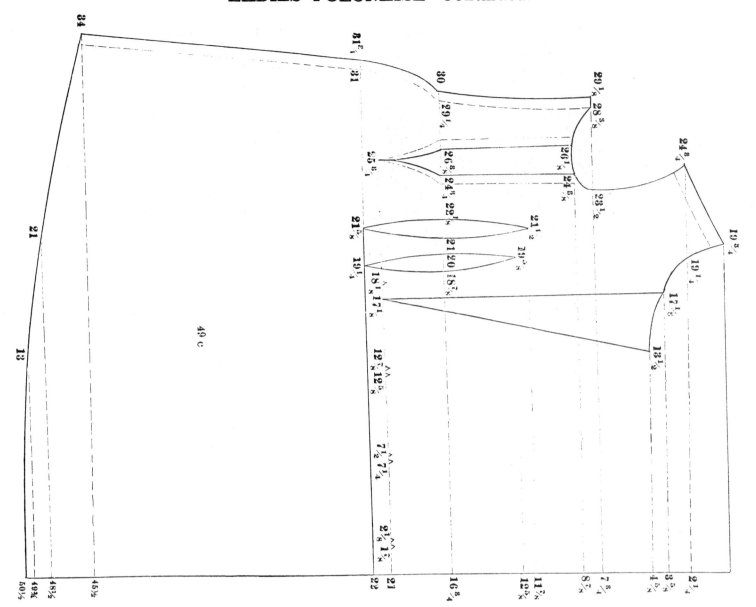

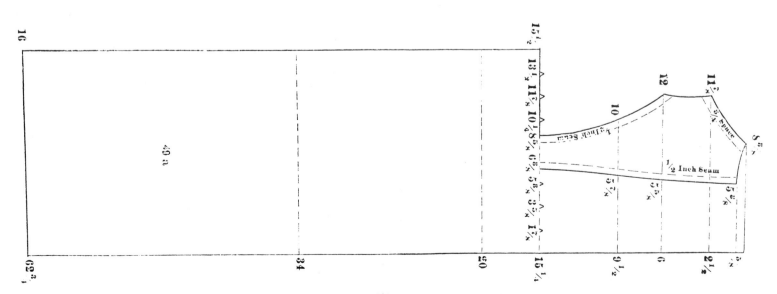

YOUNG MISSES' PLAITED WAIST AND KILT SKIRT.

Use scale corresponding with the bust measure.

It is in seven pieces: Front, back, collar, half of belt, cuff and two sleeve portions. This is a box-plaited waist. Each plait is marked. The box plaits are not sewed down to the bottom, as you can see on the diagram. In the back they are sewed down to 16¼, and in the front they are sewed down to 16¾. This fitted to the form same as any other waist. Use diagram given in the Lawn Tennis Costume for the Kilt Skirt or any other design.

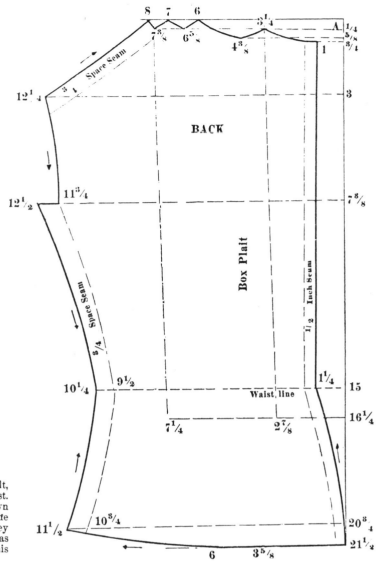

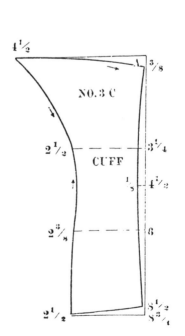

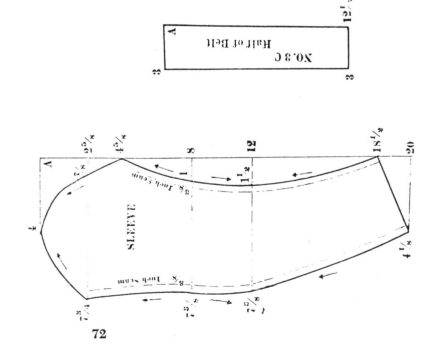

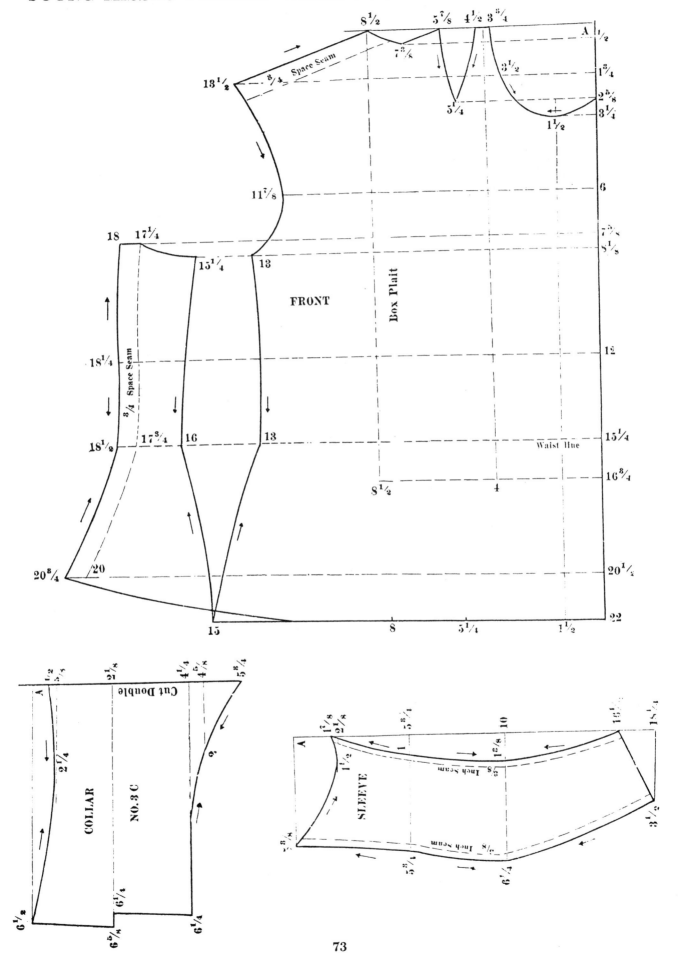

LADIES' STREET JACKET.

Use scale corresponding with the bust measure.
It consists of nine pieces: Front, Back, Side
Back, Under-arm Gore, Collar, Hood, Cuff, and
two sleeve portions.

This is a very stylish jacket. Can be made of
material to match suit or of contrasting material
according to fancy of wearer.

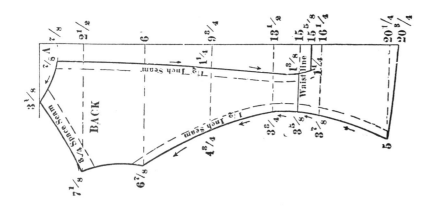

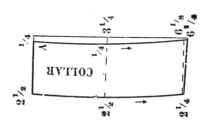

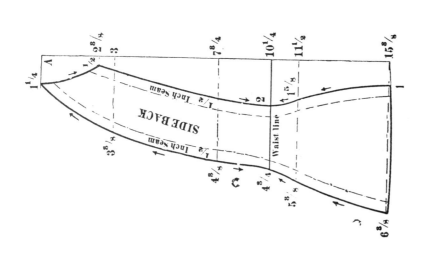

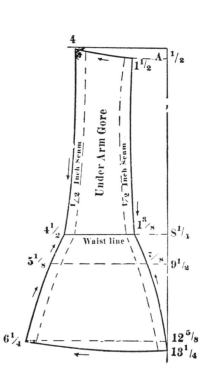

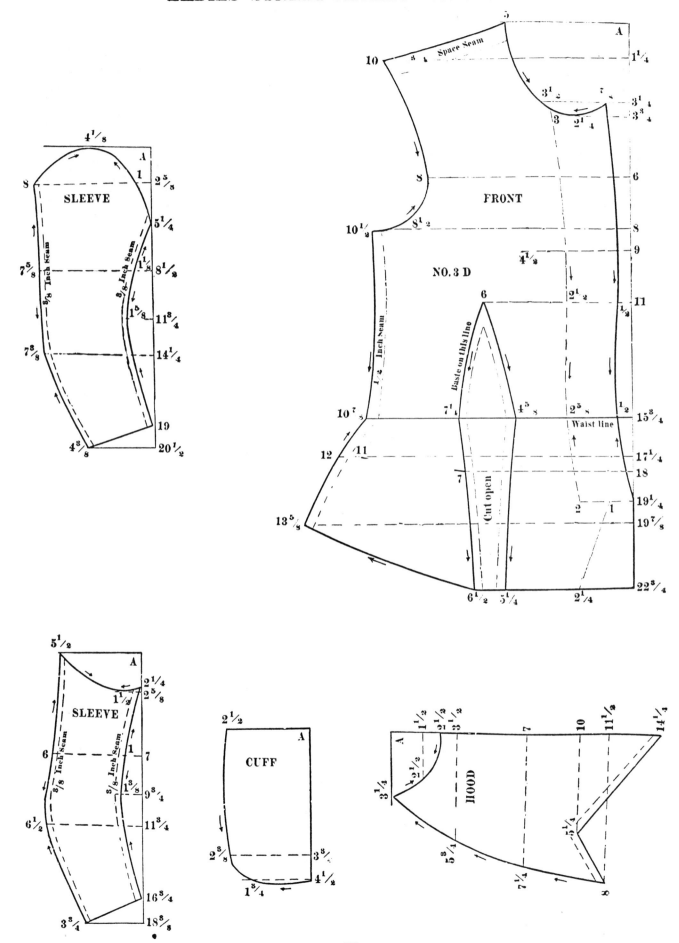

CHILD'S APRON.

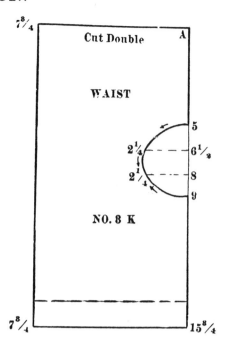

Use scale corresponding with bust measure.

Is in two pieces: One-half of Waist and one-half of Skirt.

Use embroidery for waist.

The skirt is gathered and sewed to the waist. The waist is closed in the back with buttons and button holes.

Make allowance for the tucks.

Regulate the length by the tape measure.

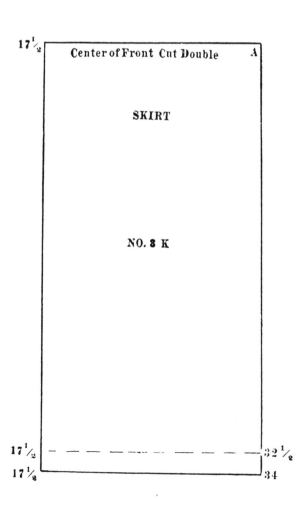

LADIES' WRAP.

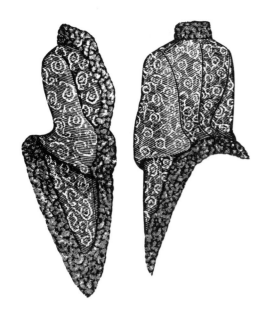

Use the scale to correspond with bust measure. Sew the sleeves in the seam between back and side back. Put parts together to correspond with the notches on the different parts. Trim to suit.

Half-inch seems are allowed.

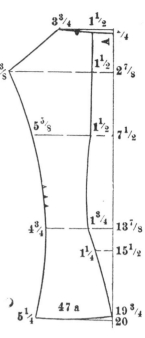

47 a

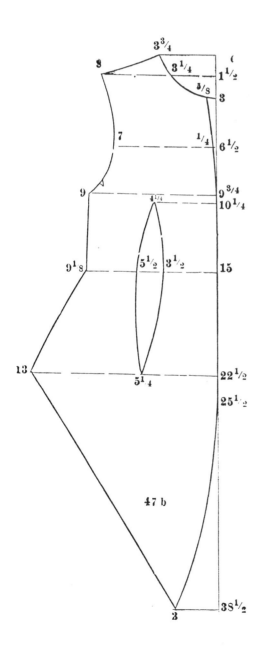

47 b

SIDE BACK

47 c

COLLAR   47 e

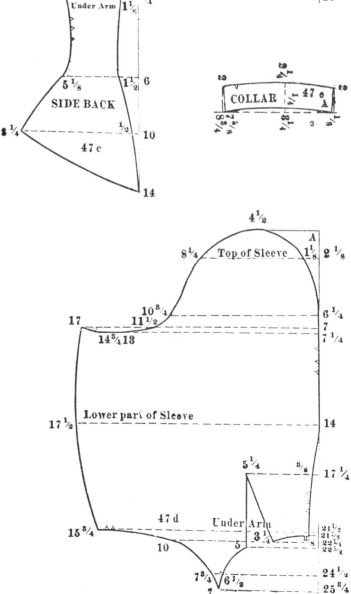

47 d

INFANT'S WRAP.

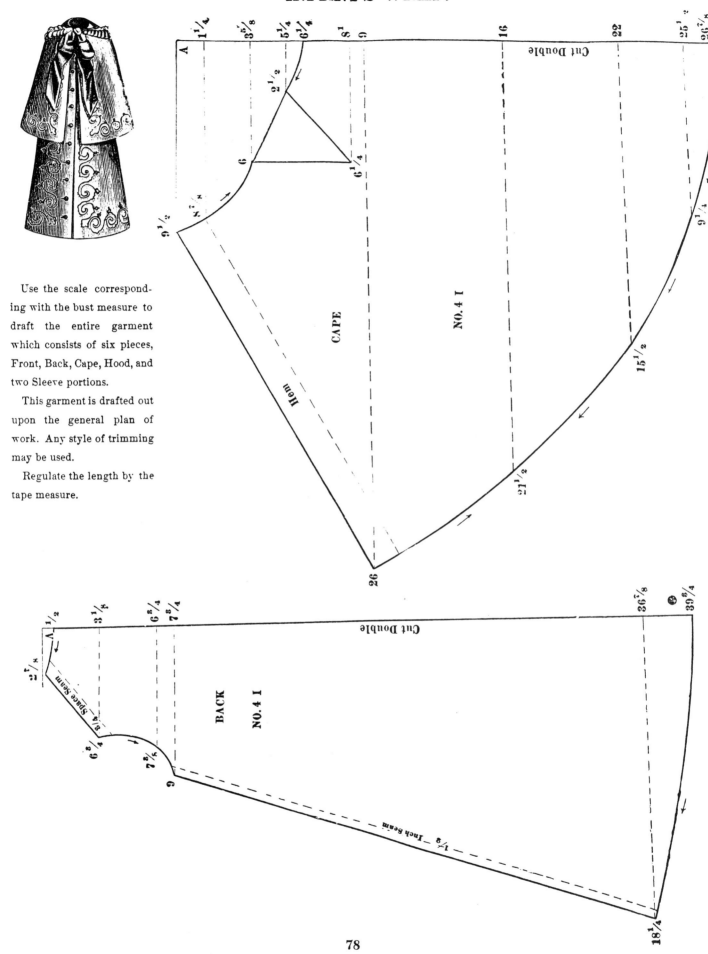

Use the scale corresponding with the bust measure to draft the entire garment which consists of six pieces, Front, Back, Cape, Hood, and two Sleeve portions.

This garment is drafted out upon the general plan of work. Any style of trimming may be used.

Regulate the length by the tape measure.

CAPE

NO. 4 I

BACK

NO. 4 I

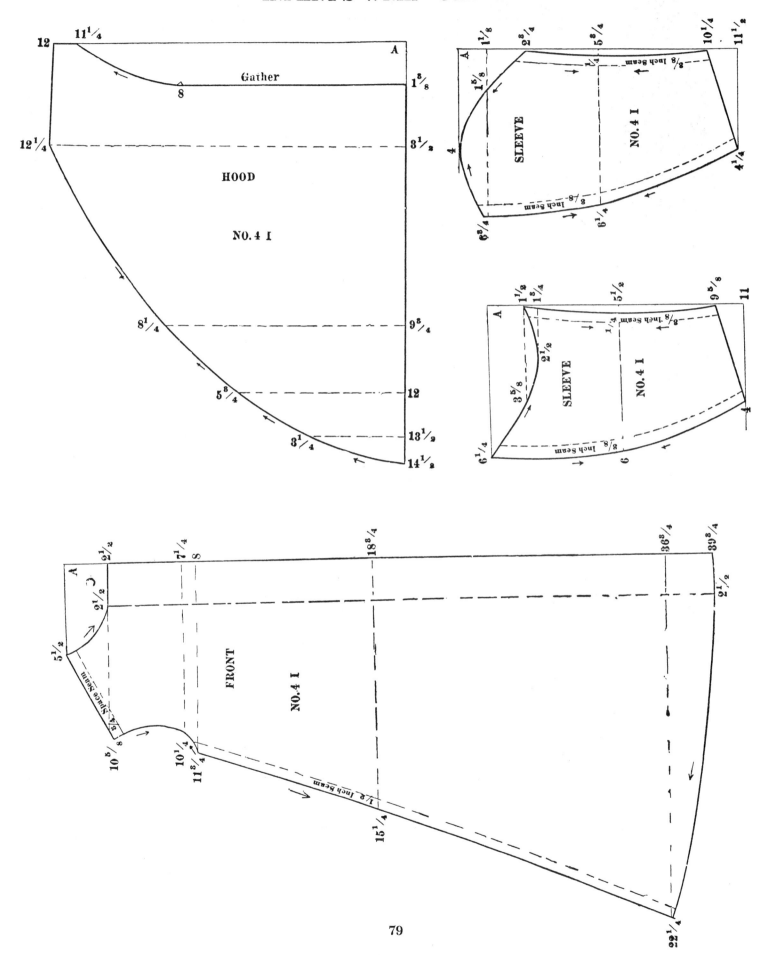

CHILD'S DRAWERS.

Use scale corresponding with waist measure.

Is in two pieces: One-half of Drawers and one-half of Waist Band. No allowance is made for the tucks.

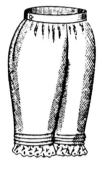

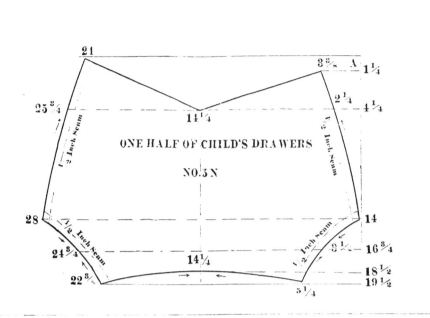

ONE HALF OF CHILD'S DRAWERS

NO.5 N

WAIST BAND NO.5 N

LADIES' SUNBONNET.

For a lady of medium size use scale 32. This is drafted as all other garments. The dotted lines across the top are to represent stitching or cording. Interline the same with two or more thicknesses: gather the back part and join to the front, connecting the notches, shirr the back part, insert a tape and draw back to suit the wearer. Any style of trimming may be used. This can be cut larger or shorter, to suit.

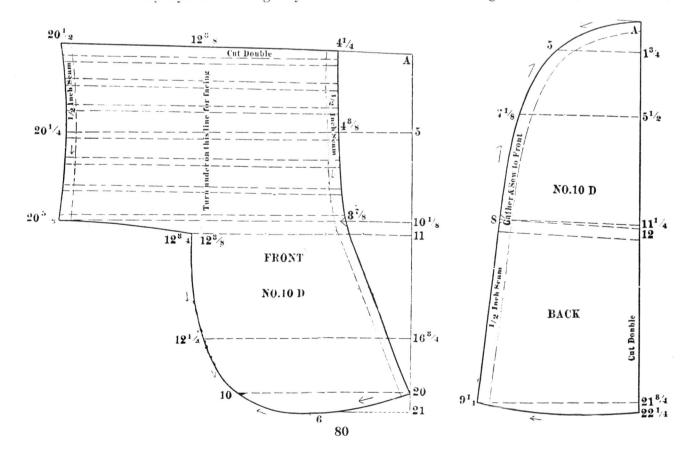

FRONT

NO.10 D

NO.10 D

BACK

CHILD'S COSTUME.

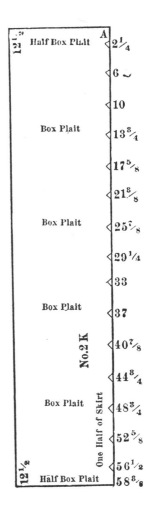

Use scale corresponding with the bust measure.

Is in five pieces: Front, Back, Vest Front, Collar, and one-half of the Skirt.

THE VEST

Can be made of the same material as the dress, and the Collar made of the contrasting material, if preferred.

THE SKIRT

Is laid in single box plaits; the trimming may be omitted.

Regulate the length by the tape measure.

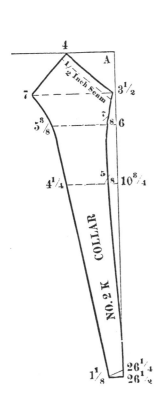

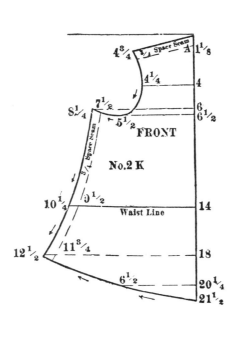

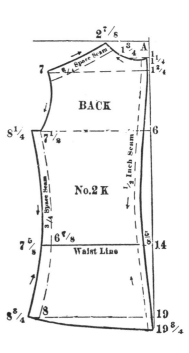

LADIES' COSTUME.

TO CUT BASQUE

Use scale corresponding with bust measure.

Is in eight pieces: Front, Back, Side Back, Under Arm Gore, Vest, Collar, and two Sleeve portions.

The vest is sewed in the first dart and in the shoulder seam, and can be made of velvet or any contrasting color.

The sleeves can be finished at the hand with a small round cuff of the same material as the vest, with very pleasing effect.

THE SKIRT

Is drafted by the waist measure, and is in four pieces: Front, Right and Left Sides, and Back Drapery.

The front is made of the same material as the vest and cuffs.

The left side consists of two double box plaits.

The right side has five side plaits turning toward the front, as shown on draft.

The straps across the front are 3¼ inches wide.

The lower one is 7 inches long, and the upper one is 5¼ inches long; cut the remaining four to correspond, and fasten on front of skirt, as shown by the figure.

First make a foundation skirt, (cut from any plain skirt pattern). Press the plaits carefully, tack with tape underneath, to stay the plaits, and fasten to foundation skirt at the waist with a band, finish bottom of foundation skirt with knife plaiting 3 inches wide.

The back drapery is laid in five plaits turning toward center of back, drape up to make bottom even.

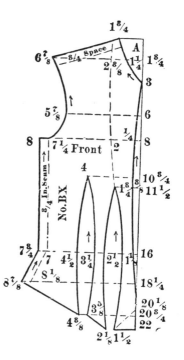

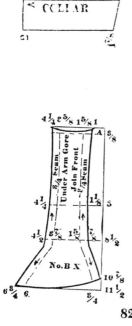

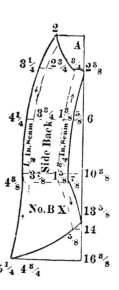

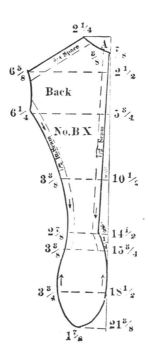

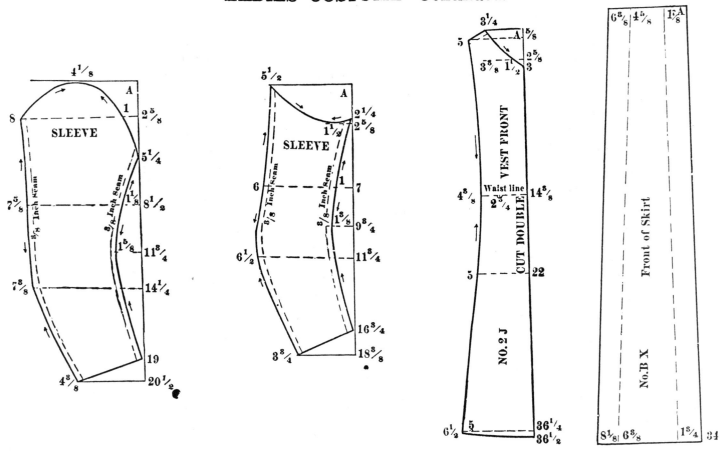

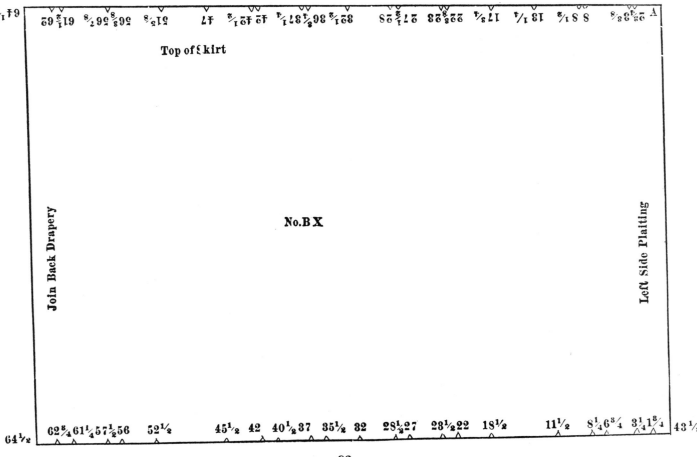

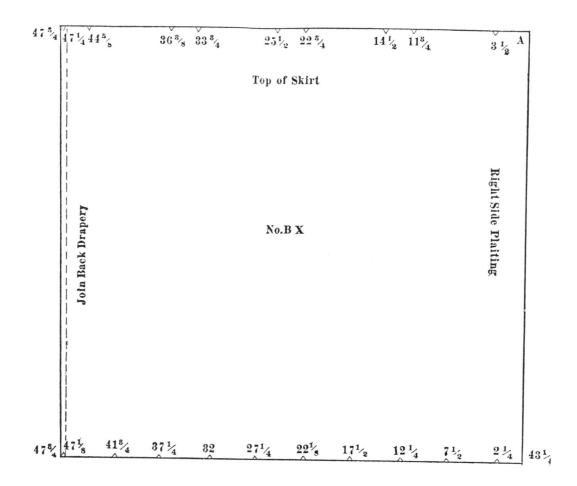

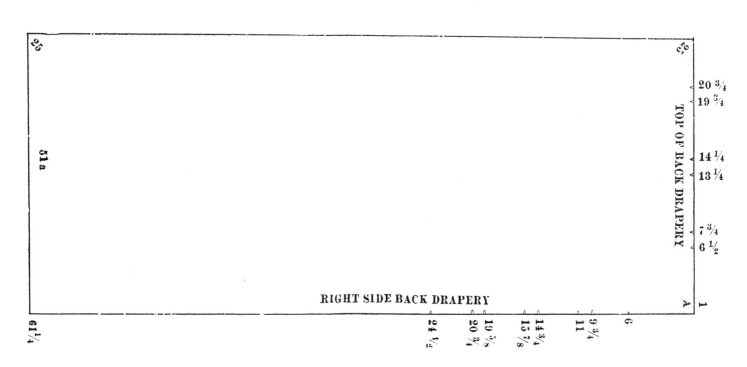

LADIES' KITCHEN APRON.

Use scale corresponding with bust measure.

Is in six pieces: Front, Back, Shoulder Strap, Belt, Pocket and Strap.

The binding should be held tight, to prevent enlarging the neck.

Regulate the length by the tape line.

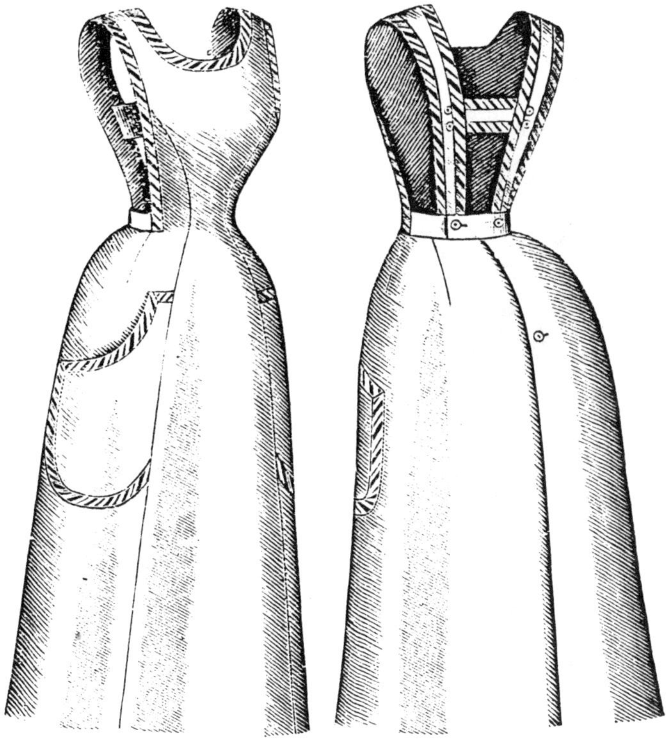

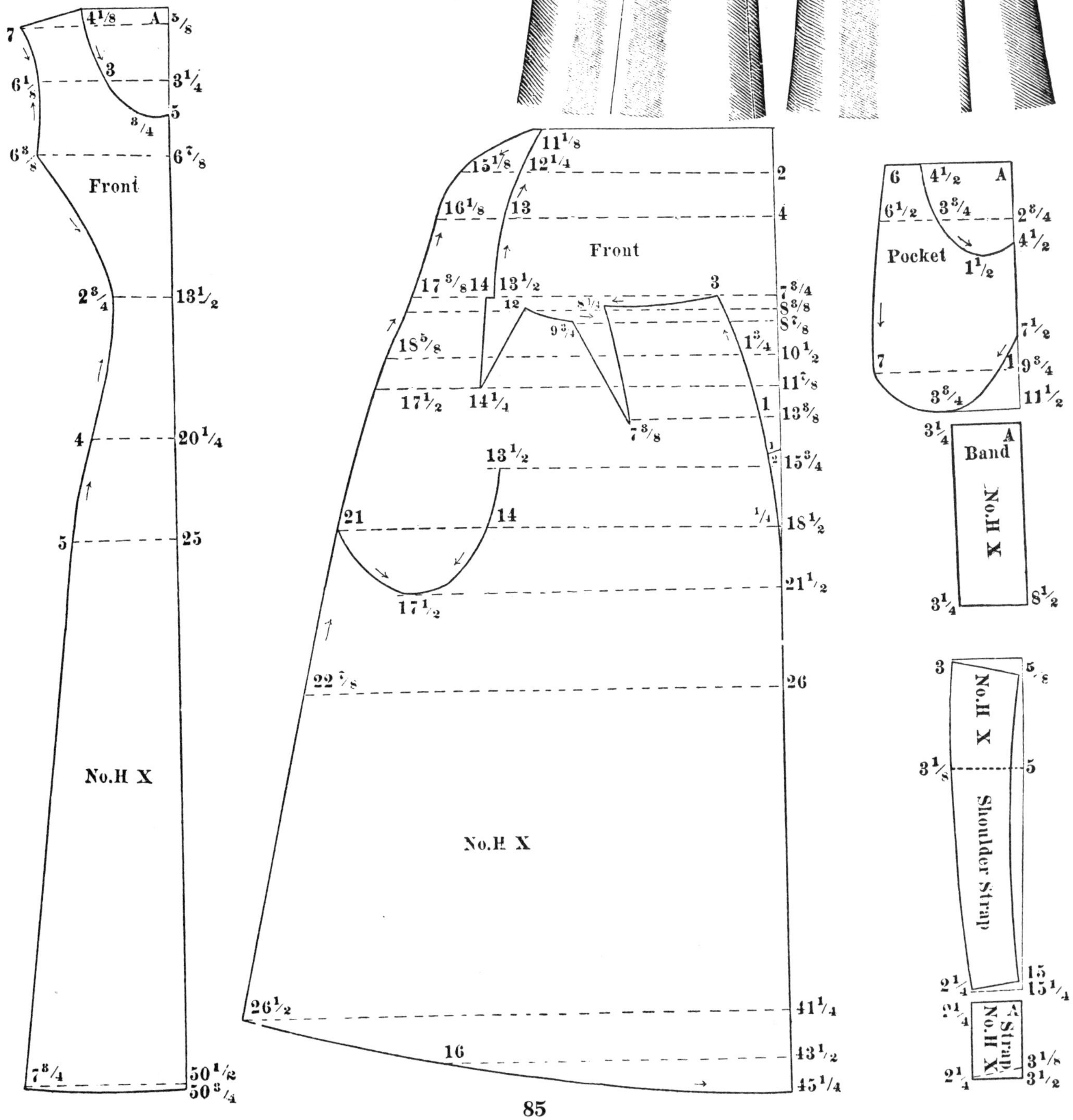

Front

No.H X

Front

No.H X

Pocket

Band

No.H X

No.H X

Shoulder Strap

Strap

No.H X

LADIES' SHORT WRAP.

Use the scale corresponding with the bust measure to draft the entire garment, which consists of four pieces: Front, Back, Collar and Sleeve.

In putting this garment together connect the corresponding notches and stars. Lay the back in two pleats. If the waist line has been lengthened or shortened, lengthen or shorten the sleeve just the same. Gather the bottom of the front and finish with bows of ribbon or fancy balls.

This wrap is suitable for early Fall or Spring wear. Can be made of any suitable material.

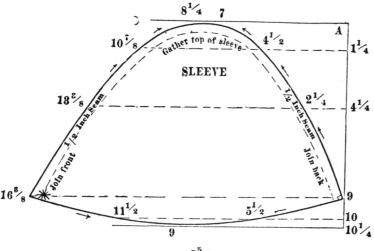

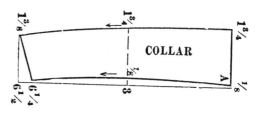

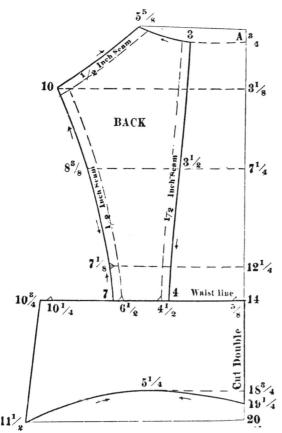

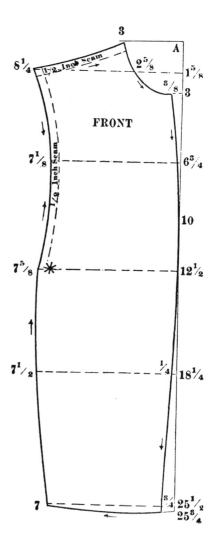

LADIES' MORNING DRESS.

Use scale corresponding with bust measure.

Is in seven pieces: Front, Back, Side Back, Back Breadth, Collar and two Sleeve portions.

Is drafted upon the general plan of work.

The back breadth is turned down two inches; gather and sew to the back on the the curved line 18¾ on base line, and the curved line on the side back 12½ on base line.

Sew the back and side back together first. The bottom can be finished with plaiting or gathered ruffles.

Regulate the length by the tape measure.

CHILD'S CLOAK.

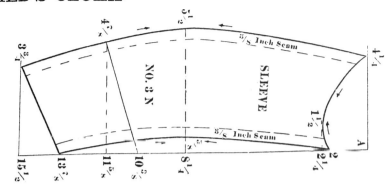

Use scale corresponding with bust measure.

Is in five pieces: Front, Back, Collar, and two Sleeve portions.

Lay two single box plaits in the back.

The front can be finished with buttons, if preferred.

Regulate the length by the tape measure.

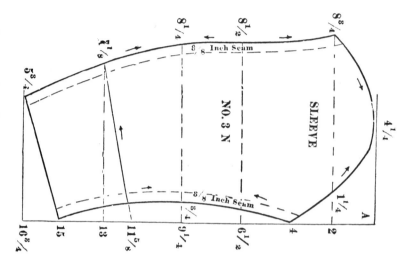

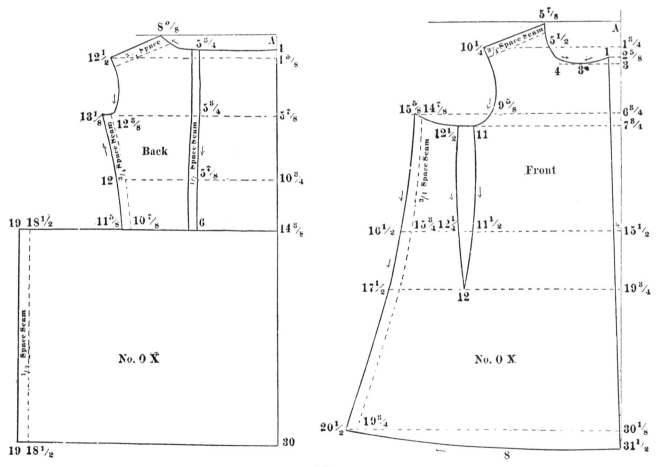

INFANTS' HIGH NECK DRESS.

Use scale corresponding with the bust measure.

Is in four pieces: Front, Back, Side Gore and Sleeve.

The upper and the under part of sleeve is drafted together as shown in draft.

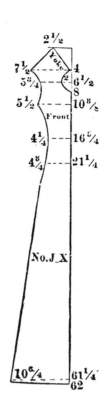

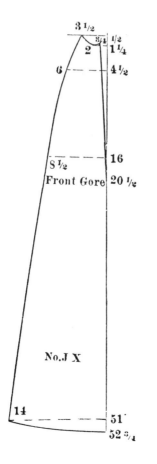

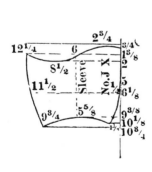

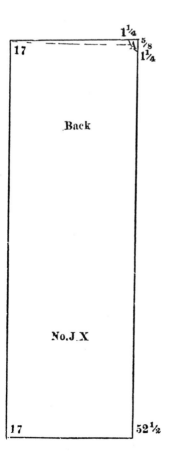

LADIES' STREET COSTUME.

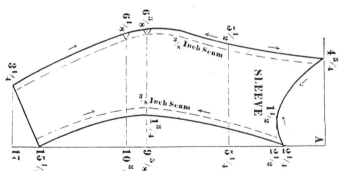

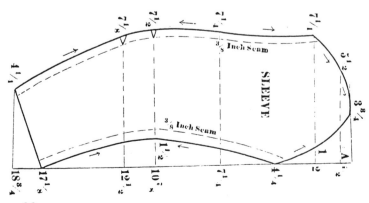

Use scale corresponding with the bust measure to draft the Polonaise.

Is in seven pieces: Front, Back, Side Back, one-half of Back Breadth, Collar and two Sleeve portions.

The back breadth is gathered and sewed to the back portion.

Lay two upward turning plaits in the front, and join to the back, bringing the plaits up over the side gore and stay it underneath.

The front is closed with buttons and button holes.

THE SKIRT

Is drafted by the scale corresponding with the waist measure.

Is in three pieces: Front, Back and Side Gore.

Regulate the length by the tape measure.

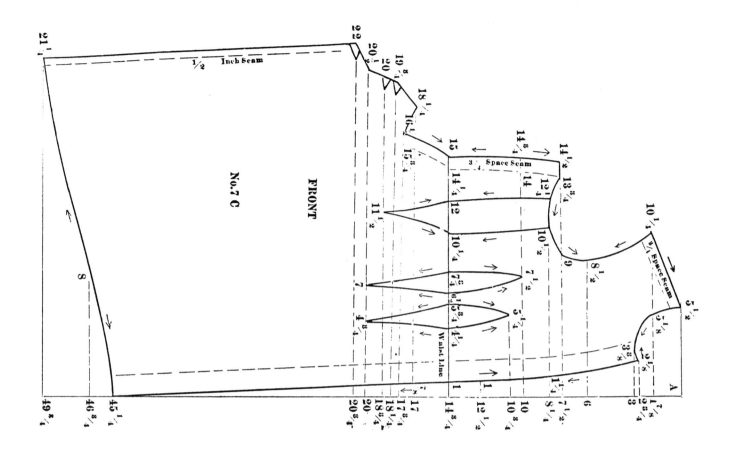

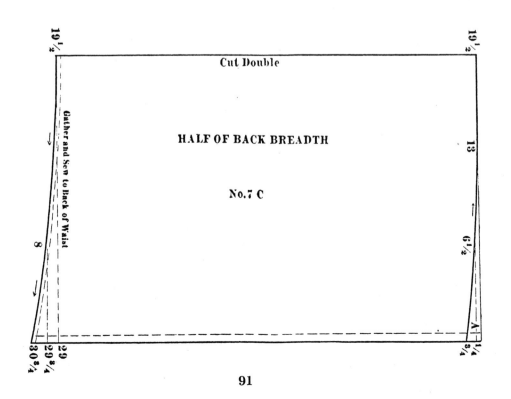

LADIES' PLAIN SKIRT.

Use the scale corresponding with the waist measure.

Is in three pieces: Front, Side Gore and Back Breadth.

This is drafted out upon the general plan of work.

Regulate the length by the tape line.

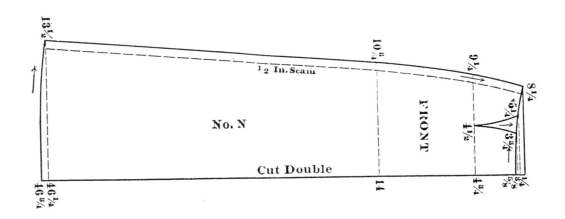

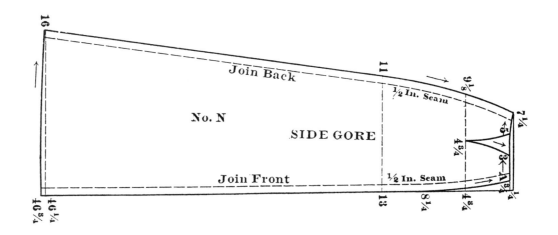

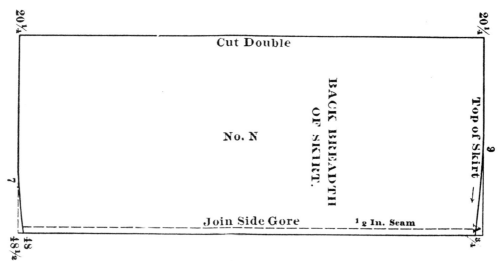

CHILD'S PRINCESS DRESS.

Use scale corresponding with the bust measure.

Is in five pieces, front, back, side back, and two sleeves.

Any style of trimming may be put upon the bottom.

Regulate the length by the tape measure.

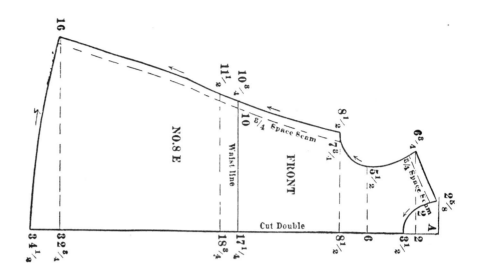

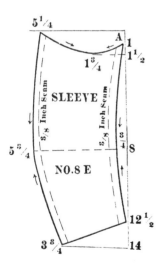

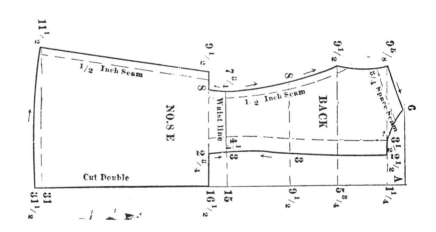

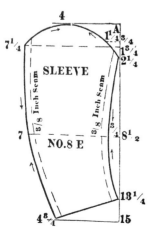

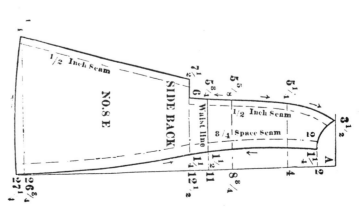

CHILD'S COSTUME.

This is a beautiful costume, suitable for either boy or girl. It is drafted by bust measure, and is in six pieces: Front, Back, Belt, Collar and two Sleeve portions.

There are three single box plaits in front and back, extending to the shoulders, and three under the arm, as shown in draft.

The plaits at top of back are marked on 2 measure line, or fourth line drawn from top, for convenience; and the plaits are marked on front on 3½ measure line, for the same reason.

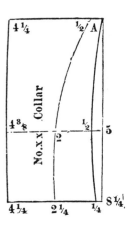

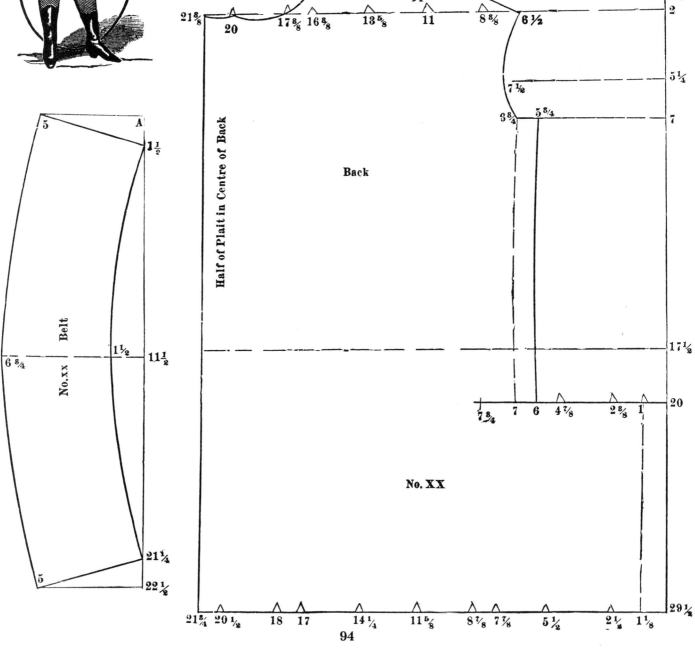

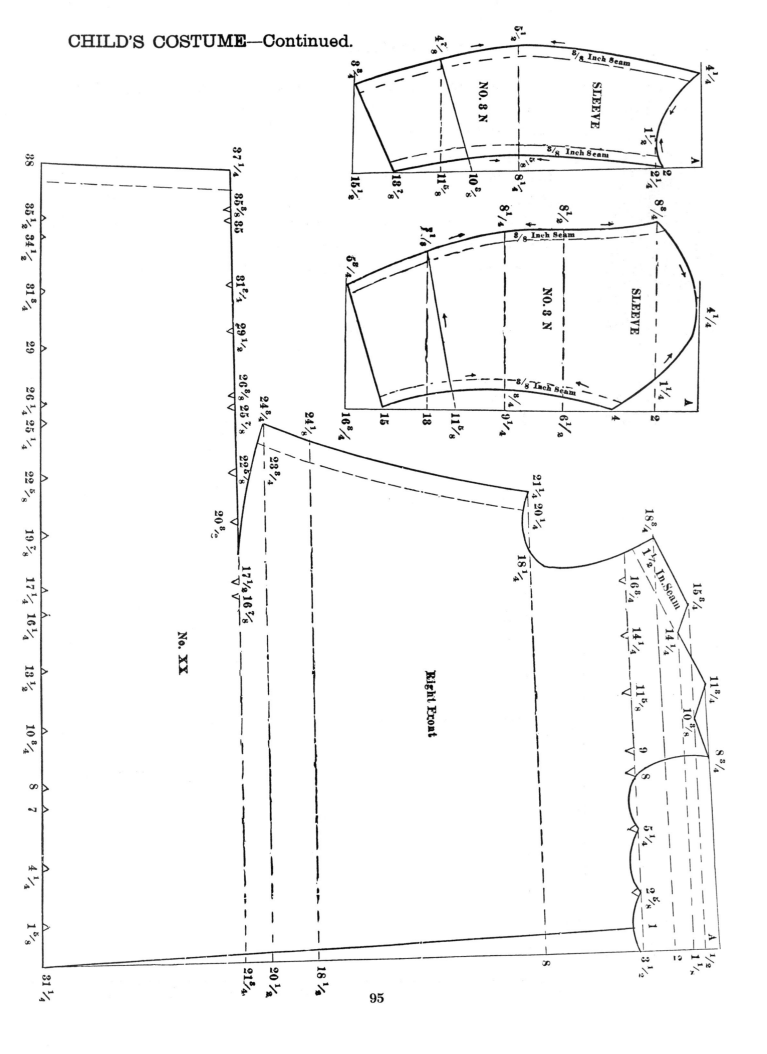

LADIES' STREET JACKET.

Use scale corresponding with bust measure.

Is in ten pieces: Jacket Front, Vest Front, Back, Side Back, Under Arm Gore, Revere for front of Jacket, Collar, Cuff and two Sleeve portions.

The Jacket can be made of any material.

Lay two double box plaits in the back.

The vest is made of velvet.

The vest front and jacket front are joined together with the under arm gore.

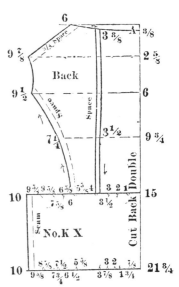

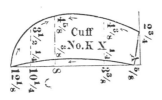

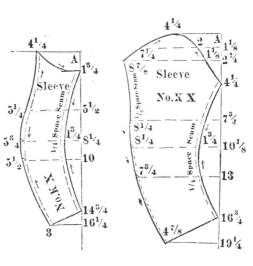

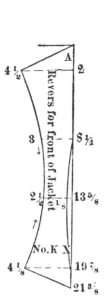

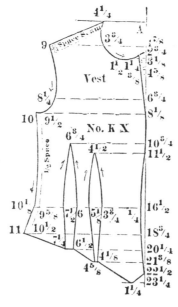

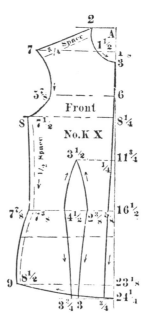

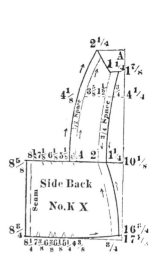

CHILD'S COSTUME.

TO CUT JACKET.

Use scale corresponding with bust measure.

Is in five pieces: Front. Back, Collar, and two Sleeve portions.

THE SKIRT

Is drafted by waist measure, and is in two pieces, half of skirt and yoke.

There are two double box plaits in skirt; 5½ are given in plate. Others are made the same.

The trimming on skirt can be omitted if desired

The length can be regulated by tape measure.

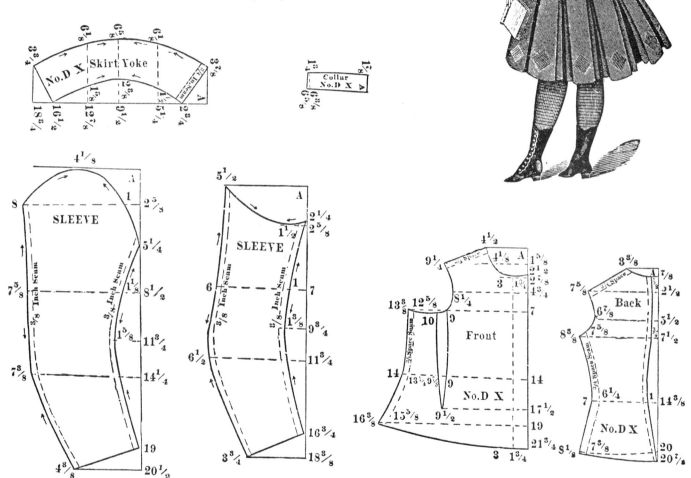

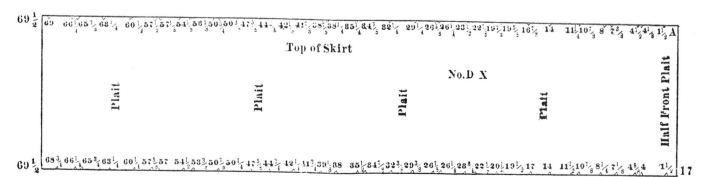

CHILD'S CLOAK.

Use scale corresponding with bust measure.

Is in eight pieces: Front, Back, one-half of Skirt, Hood, Collar, and two Sleeve portions.

This is a very fashionable Cloak, and can be made of any material.

The Skirt is cut long, and can be plaited if preferred.

The Cuffs, Collar, and Hood lining is made of velvet.

Regulate the length by the use of the tape line.

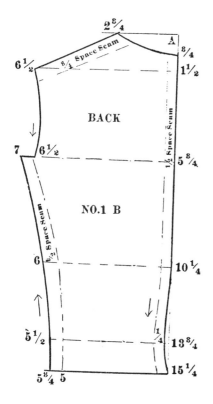

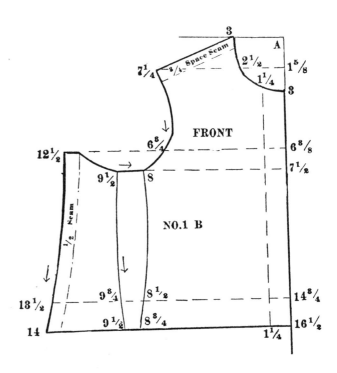

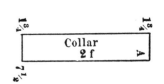

98

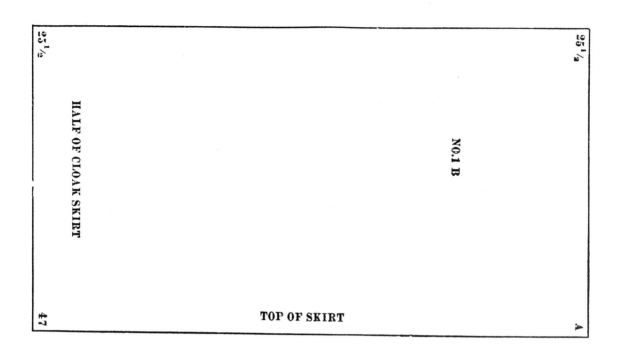

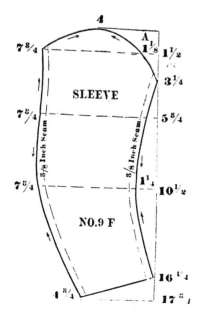

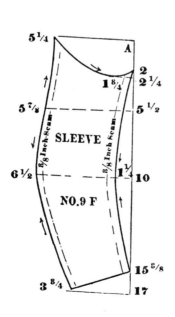

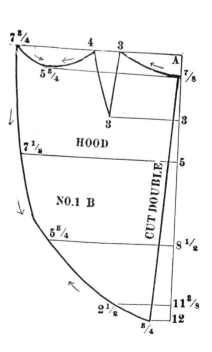

GIRL'S APRON.

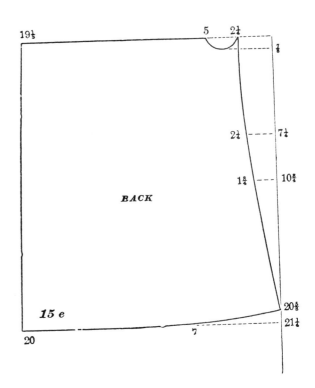

This garment is laid off by the bust measure, and in accordance with the general directions. It is in five pieces: Front, Back, Yoke, Pocket and Sash. Gather across the top of the back and join it to the yoke from one end of each portion of the sash, and insert it in the under-arm seams, as shown by notches. Turn a lap on the pocket, and attach it in proper place. Any style of trimming may be used. One space seam is allowed on shoulder and under-arm seams; one-fourth inch on all others.

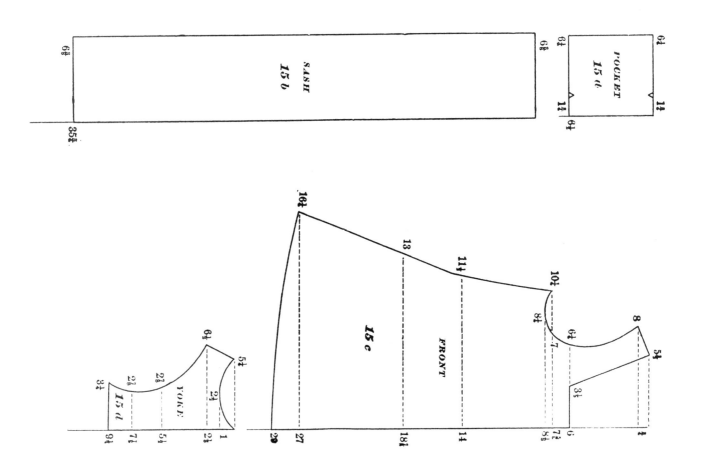

100

LADIES' NEWMARKET, WITH CAPE.

This is again shown on page 58.

The Cape and Rolling Collar are given on this page, and drafted by the scale corresponding with the bust measure.

This Cape can be made of fur, Astrachan cloth or of the same material as the Newmarket.

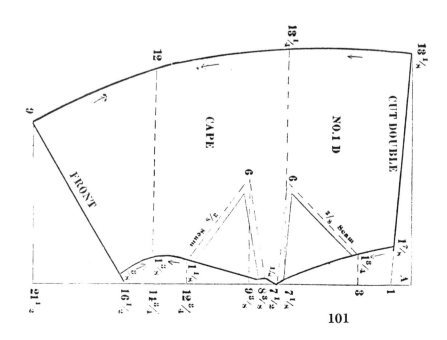

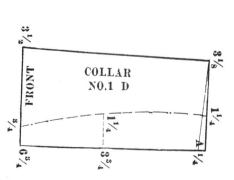

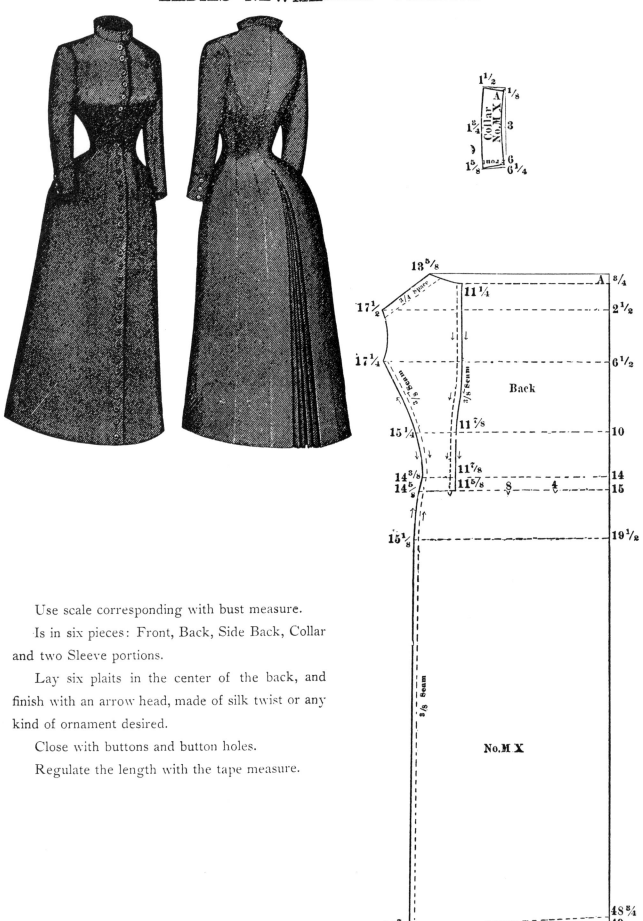

Use scale corresponding with bust measure.

Is in six pieces: Front, Back, Side Back, Collar and two Sleeve portions.

Lay six plaits in the center of the back, and finish with an arrow head, made of silk twist or any kind of ornament desired.

Close with buttons and button holes.

Regulate the length with the tape measure.

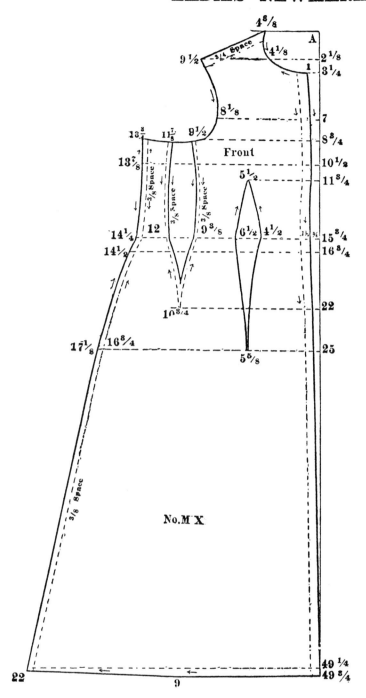

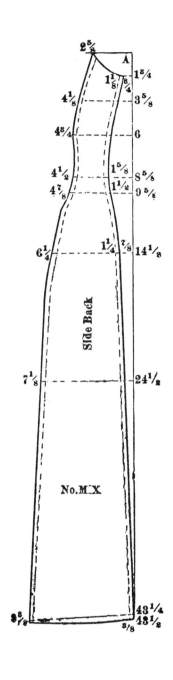

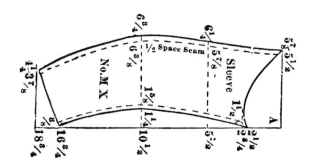

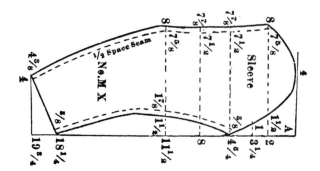

103

LADIES' WRAP.

Use scale corresponding with bust measure.

Is in five pieces: Front, Back, Under Arm Gore, Collar and Sleeve.

Draft upon the general plan.

Connect waist lines in putting the garment together.

Fold the sleeve at the figure 13¾ on base line, designated by a star, after which join it to the back. Join to the star on the cross measure line running from 15½ on base line.

Between the two stars at the top of the sleeve on cross measure line running from 1½ on base line are to be gathered.

Follow the arrows closely in drafting.

There is one double box plait in the center of the back.

Any style of an ornament can be used.

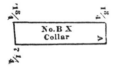

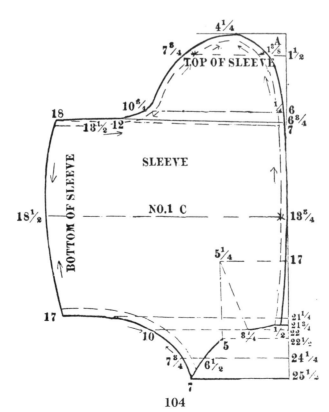

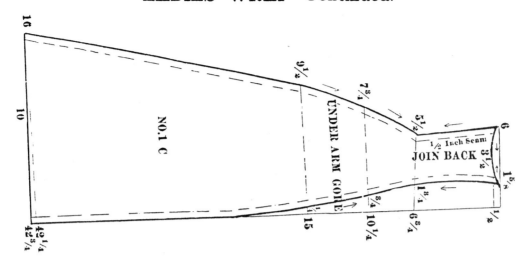

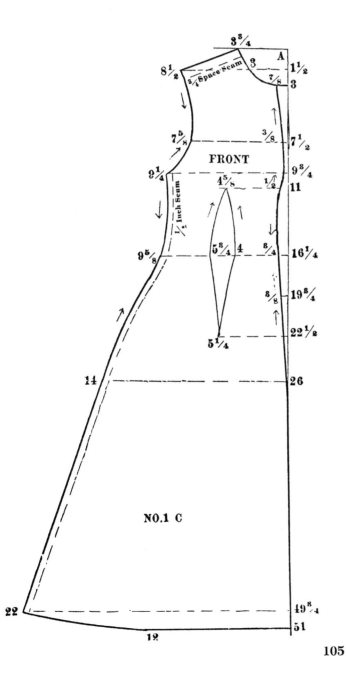

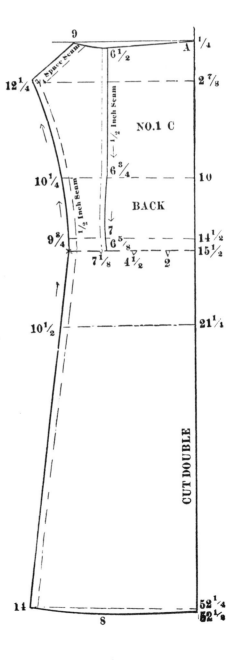

LADIES' STREET COSTUME.

Use scale corresponding with the bust measure.

Is in six pieces: Right and Left Front, Back, Collar and two Sleeve portions.

This is a beautiful Polonaise, and easily drafted if care is taken to follow the arrows closely.

Each plait is marked.

The left front has seven upward-turning plaits.

The right front has three upward-turning plaits.

These two fronts are drafted separately, but the material of which the Polonaise is to be made should be cut double to avoid a seam down the front.

The waist is left open down to the figures 25 on base line.

The back and side back are drafted together.   The extra fullness in the back is laid in plaits.

There are two loops, one on each side.

The back is draped up until it becomes even at the bottom of the skirt.

THE SKIRT

Is cut from the plain skirt given in this issue.   Any style of trimming may be used upon the skirt.

Regulate the length by the use of the tape measure.

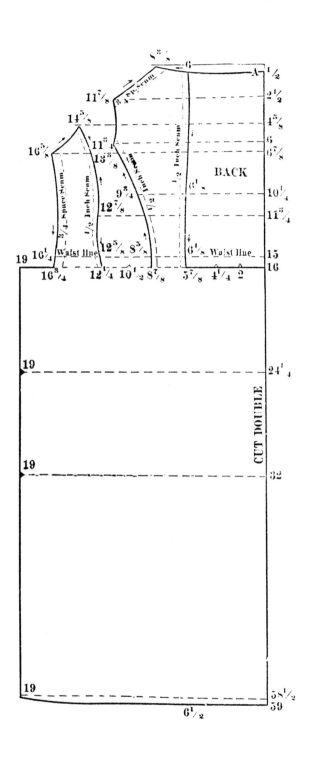

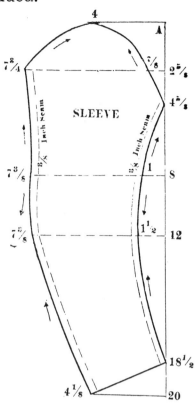

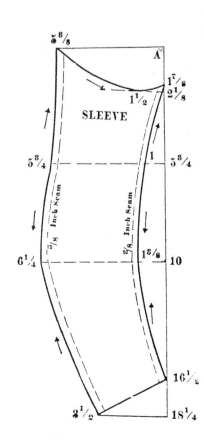

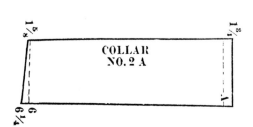

COLLAR
NO. 2 A

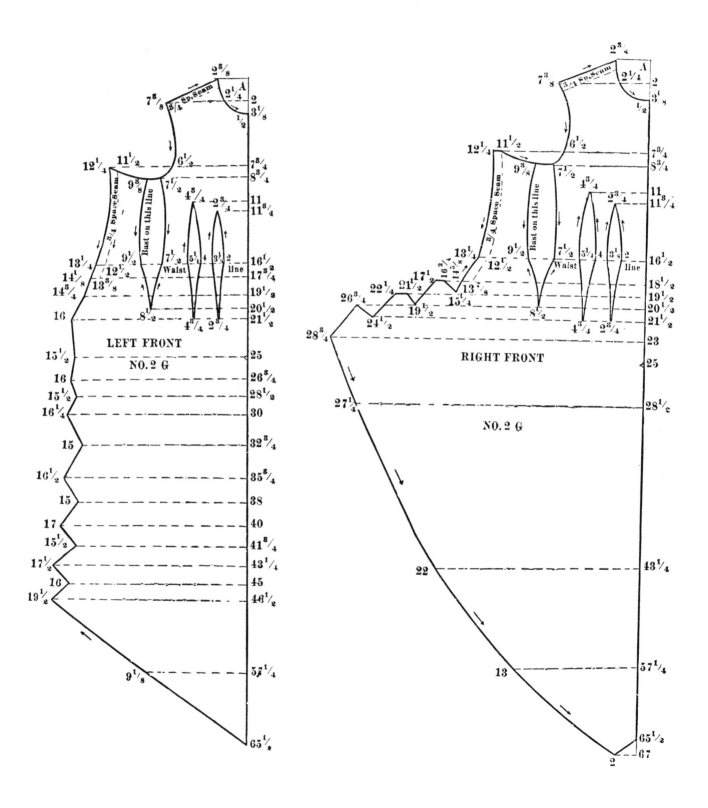

CHILD'S APRON.

Use scale corresponding with the bust measure.

It is in two pieces: one-half of Front and Tie.

Ribbon can be used for the ties, if preferred.

Regulate the length by the tape measure.

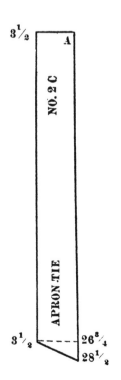

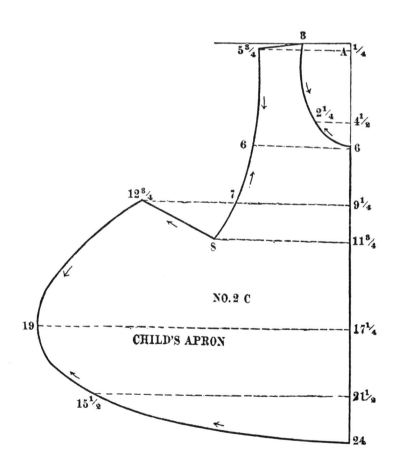

NO. 2 C

CHILD'S APRON

CHILD'S STREET COSTUME.

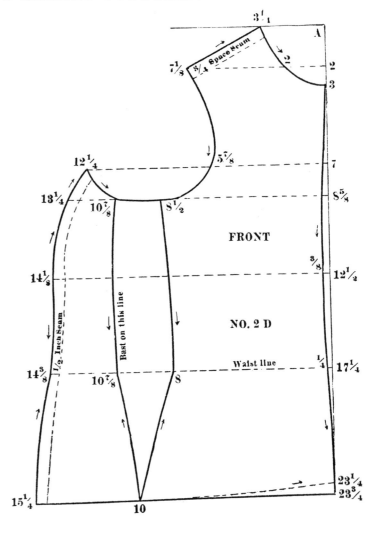

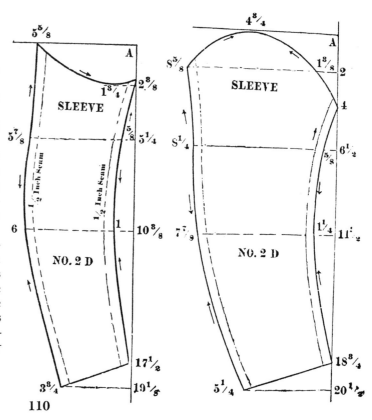

Use scale corresponding with the bust measure.

Is in seven pieces: Upper and Under Fronts, Back and Front, Collar and two Sleeve portions.

This is drafted upon the general plan of work.

The Front and Side Back are drafted together.

Baste the front and back together; get the desired length for the skirt by the tape measure. It is a straight piece of goods, can be either laid in plaits or gathered. This costume is gathered. The back is finished with a large bow of ribbon.

The upper front is shirred on 24 cross-measure line, and sewed to the under front on 21½ cross-measure line. The upper front is gathered at the neck to fit under front. The right side is fastened firmly to the front. The garment is closed on the left side with hooks and eyes. Lace may be used instead of embroidery, if desired. Regulate the length by the use of tape measure.

110

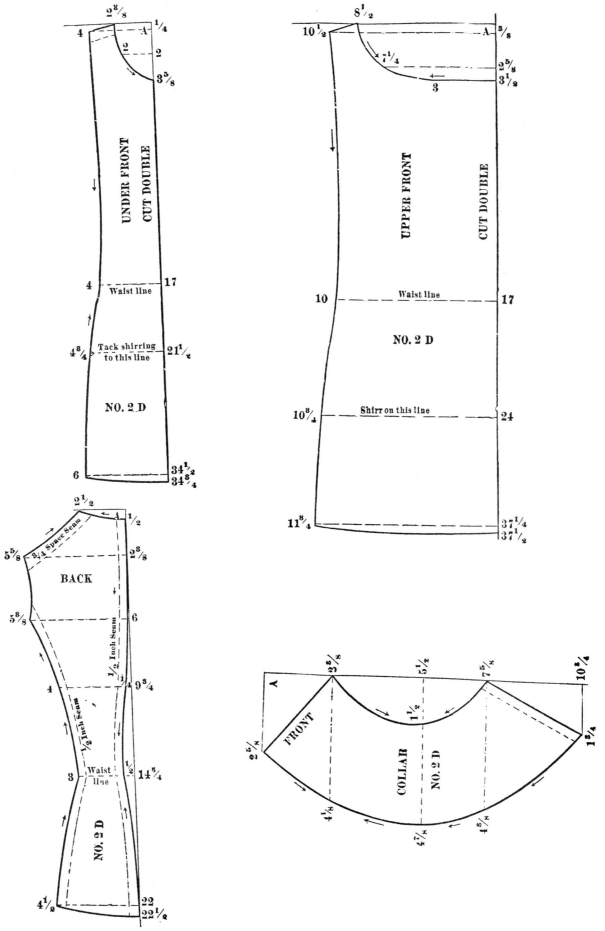

111

CHILD'S WRAPPER.

Use the scale corresponding with the bust measure to draft the entire garment.

It consists of five pieces: Front, Back, Side Back, Collar and two Sleeve portions.

Lay the extra fullness in the back in three side pleats, turning toward the center of back. Cut the cloth double to avoid a seam.

Tuck the front as represented.

Lay the front edge of the pattern on the straight edge of the goods.

Regulate the length by the use of the tape measure.

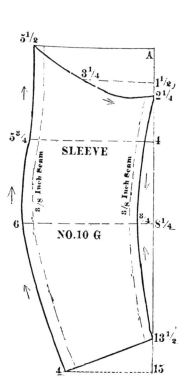

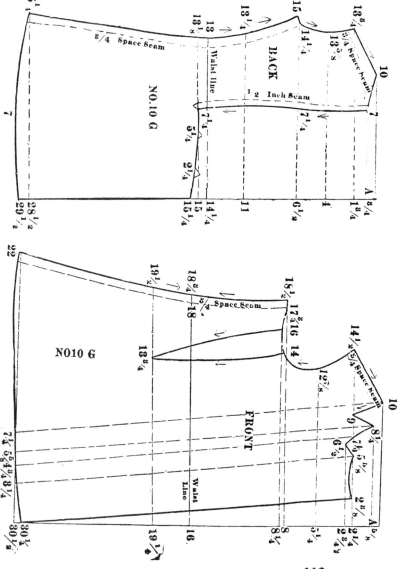

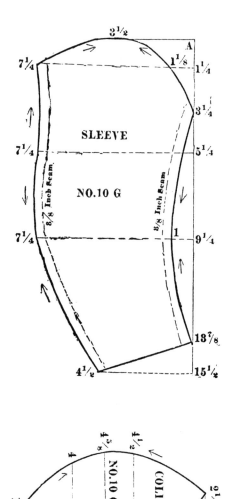

LADIES' SHORT WRAP.

Use scale corresponding with the bust measure.

Is in five pieces: Front, Back, Underarm Gore, Collar and Sleeve.

Follow the arrows closely. Connect the waist lines and join the notches.

Close in front with hooks and eyes.

Any style of trimming may be used.

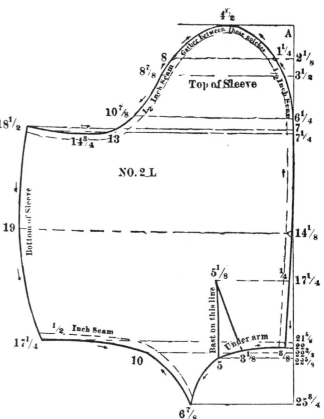

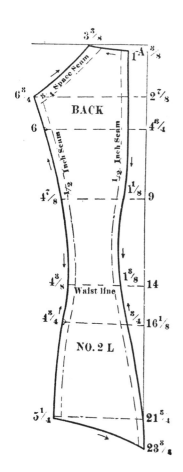

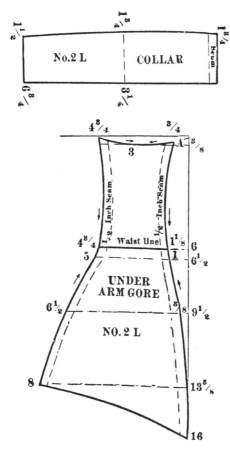

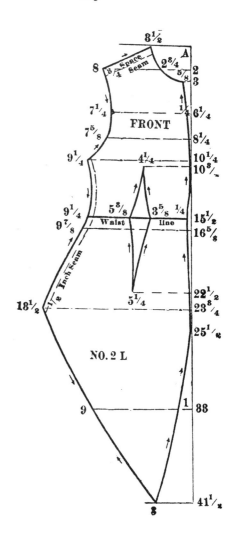

CHILD'S CLOAK.

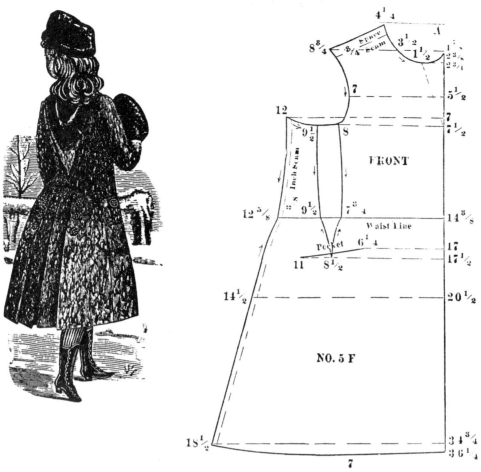

FRONT

NO. 5 F

Use scale corresponding with the bust measure.

Is in eight pieces: Front, Back, Side Back, Collar, Cuff, Hood, and two Sleeve portions. Lay the plaits in Back and Side Back according to the notches. Gather the hood at the top and bottom.

Regulate the length by the use of the tape measure.

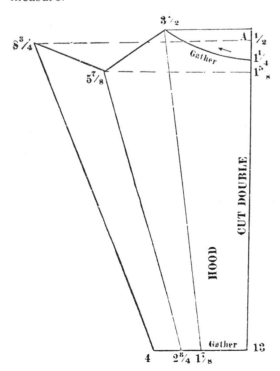

HOOD CUT DOUBLE

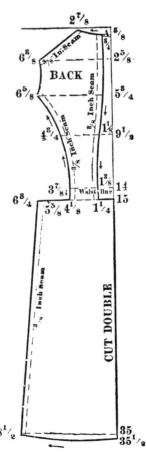

BACK

CUT DOUBLE

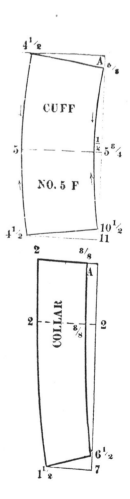

CUFF

NO. 5 F

COLLAR

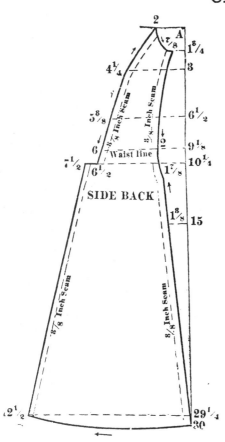

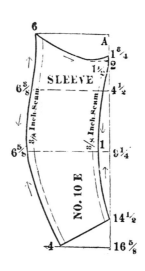

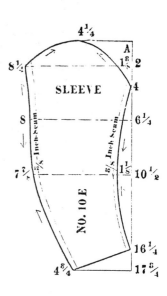

CHILD'S COSTUME.

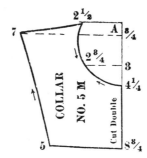

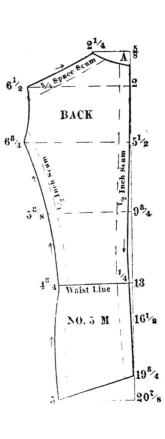

To draft Jacket, Vest and Sleeves, use scale corresponding with the bust measure.

Is in eight pieces: two Fronts, two Backs, Collar, two Sleeve portions, and one-half of Skirt.

This is drafted upon the general plan of work.

The Skirt is drafted by the scale corresponding with the waist measure. Lay plaits according to the notches.

Regulate the length by the use of the tape measure.

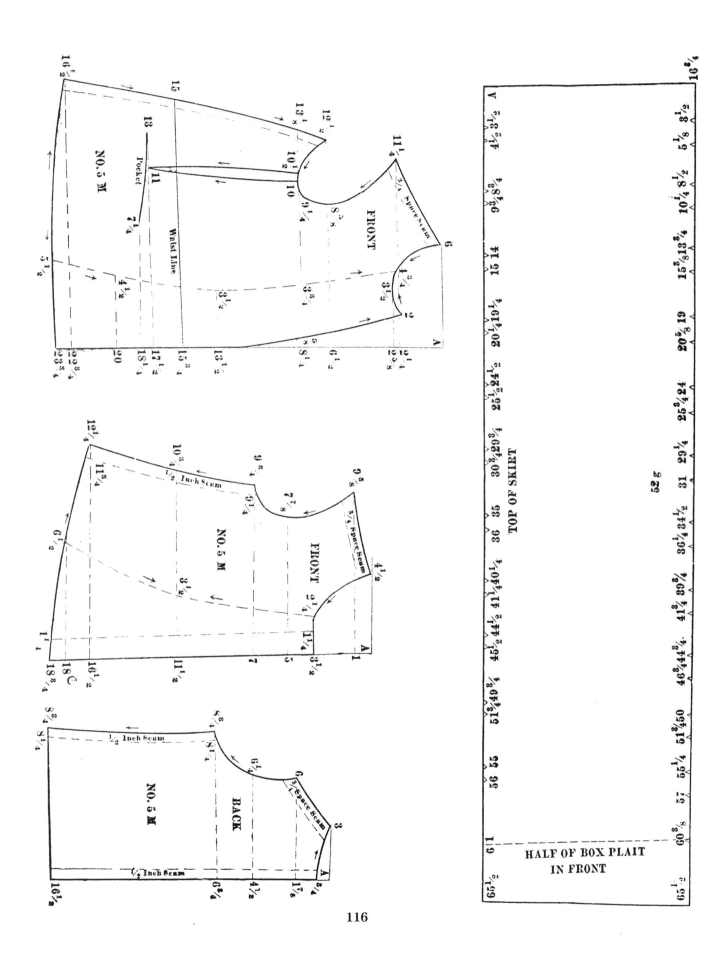

LADIES' CHEMISE.

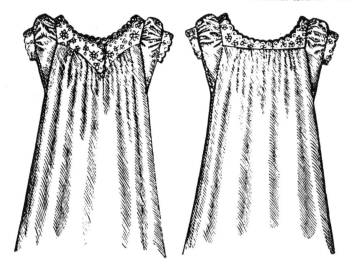

Use scale corresponding with bust measure.

Is in six pieces: Front, Back, Front Yoke, Back Yoke, Band and Sleeve.

Regulate the length by the tape measure.

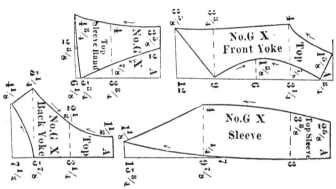

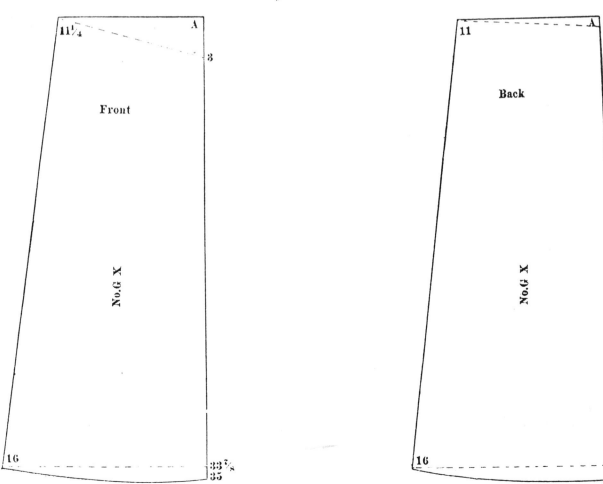

CHILD'S COMBINATION UNDERGARMENT.

Use scale corresponding with the bust measure.

Is in three pieces: Front, Back and Sleeve.

Is drafted out upon the general plan of work.

Follow the arrows closely.

No allowance is made for the tucks.

Regulate the length by the use of the tape measure.

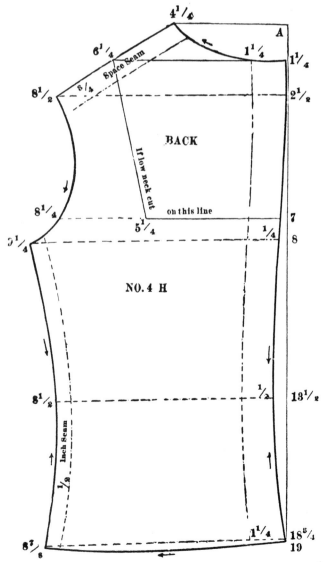

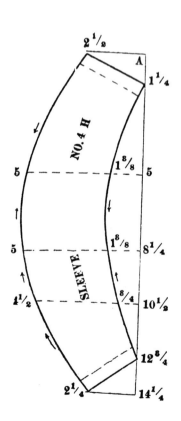

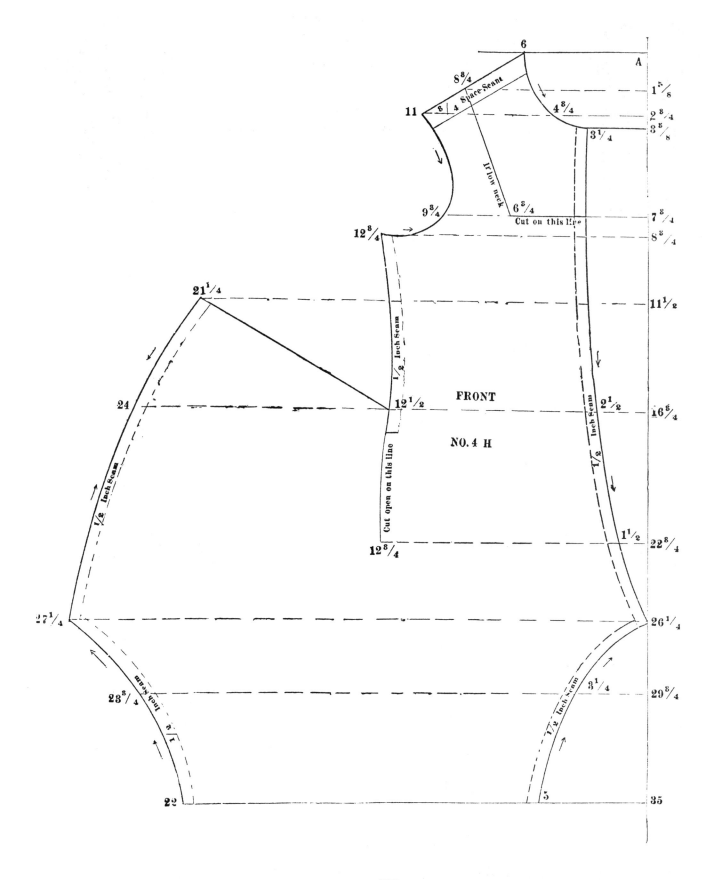

LADIES' STREET COSTUME.

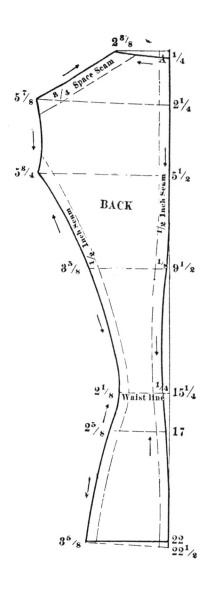

TO DRAFT BASQUE.

Use scale corresponding with the bust measure.

Is in eight pieces: Front, Back, Side Back, two Under Arm Gores, Collar and two Sleeve portions.

This is a French Basque, of which there is such a demand at present, and gives the most perfect shape to the figure for which we are fitting of any basque we have.

The front may be turned away and insert a vest if preferable, and also allowance may be made for plaits in the back.

THE SLEEVES

May be finished with a cuff at the hand if desired.

THE DRAPERY.

Use scale corresponding with the waist measure.

Is in two pieces: Front and Back, and is laid in plaits as shown on the figure. The pattern for the wrap is given in this issue, and is a very stylish and dressy wrap.

THE SKIRT.

Is cut from the plain skirt pattern given in this issue. Regulate the length by the use of the tape measure.

The diagrams for the wrap are given on page 124

LADIES' STREET COSTUME—Continued.

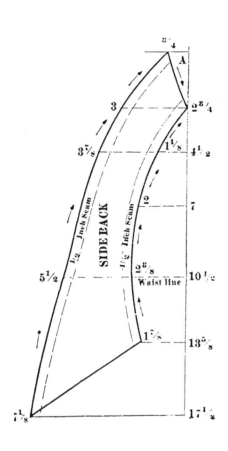

SIDE BACK

3/4

A

3   2 3/4

3 7/8   1 1/8   4 1/2

1/2 Inch Seam

1/2 Inch Seam

2   7

5 1/2   2 3/8   Waist line   10 1/2

1 5/8   13 5/8

7 1/8   17 1/2

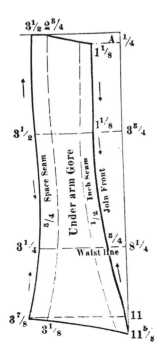

3 1/2   2 3/4

A   1/4

1 1/8

Under arm Gore

Space Seam

Inch Seam

Join Front

3 1/2   1 1/8   3 3/4

3/4

1/2

3 1/4   3/4   8 1/4

Waist line

3 7/8

3 1/8   11

11 5/8

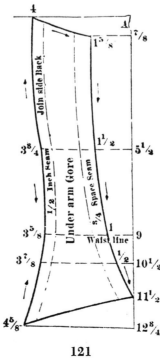

4

A   7/8

1 5/8

Join side Back

1/2 Inch Seam

Under arm Gore

Space Seam

3 3/4   1 1/2   5 1/2

3 5/8   1   9

Waist line

3 7/8   1/2   10 1/2

11 1/2

4 5/8   12 3/4

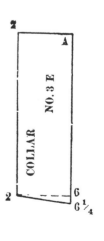

2   A

COLLAR   NO. 3 E

2   6

6 1/4

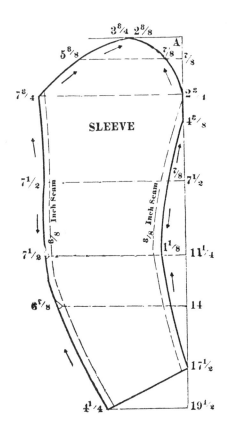

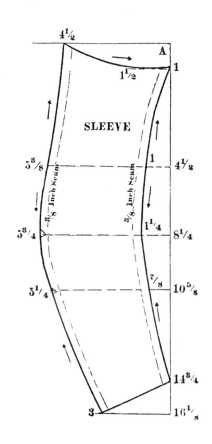

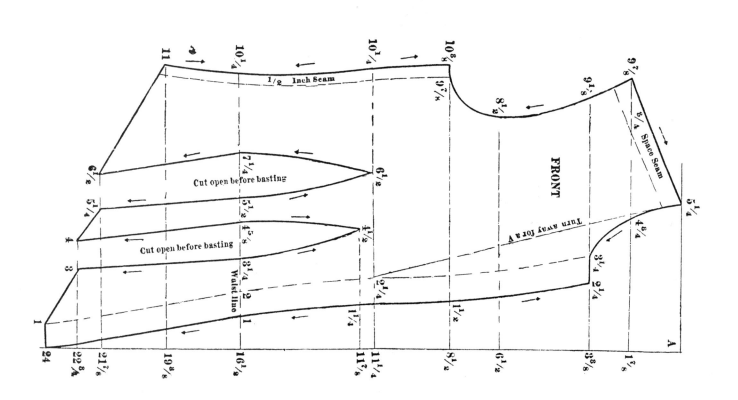

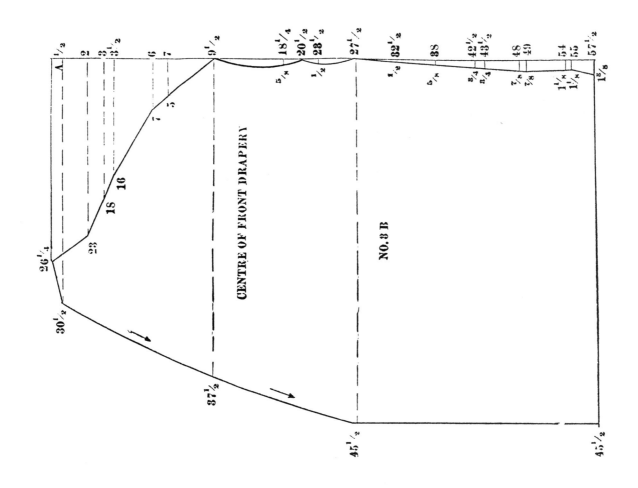

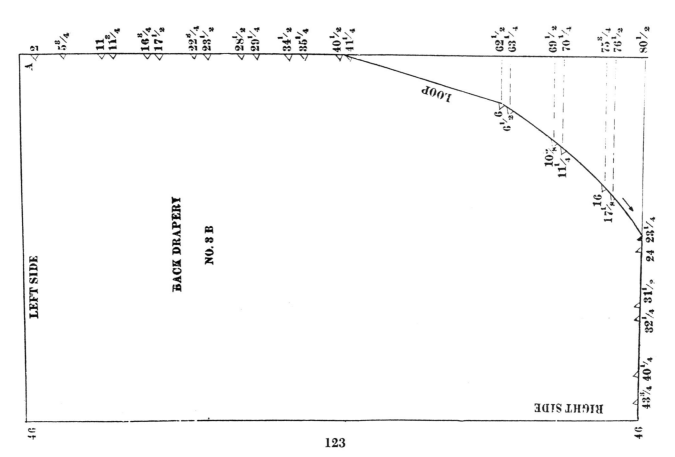

LADIES' WRAP.

Use scale corresponding with bust measure.

It consists of four pieces: Front, Back, Sleeve and Collar.

This is drafted upon the general plan of work.

Watch the arrows closely.

Join together according to the notches.

The sleeves are loose.

Any style of trimming may be used, and almost any material.

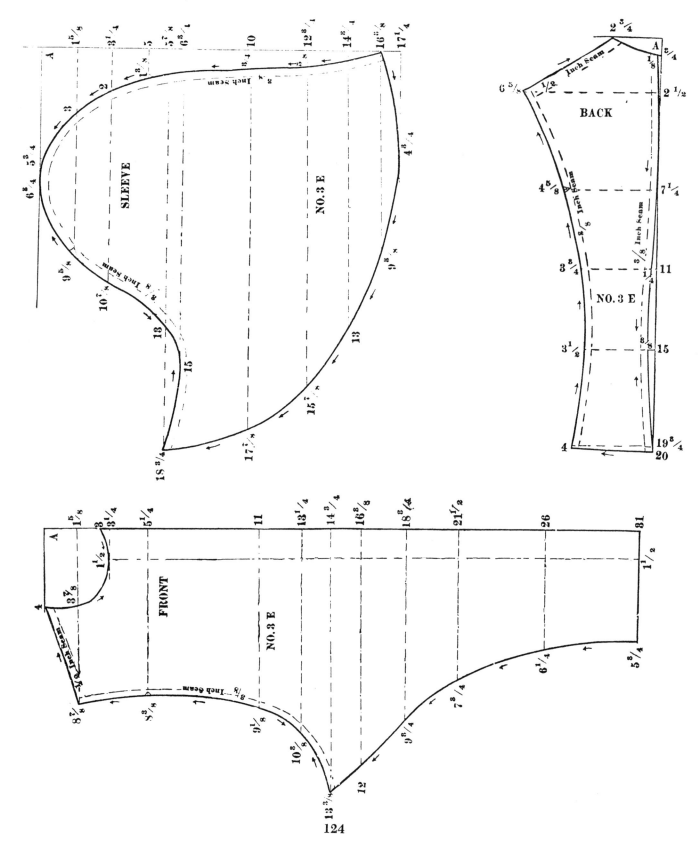

CHILD'S STREET COSTUME.

Use scale corresponding with the bust measure.

Is in ten pieces: Right and Left Front, Yoke and Shirring for Front, Back, Side Back, Collar, two Sleeve portions, and one-half of box-plaited Skirt.

THE FRONT.

The dotted line running from $3\frac{1}{4}$ on first cross measure line down to $4\frac{1}{8}$ on bottom line is the lining for the yoke and shirring for vest. After the shirring for the vest is gathered at top and sewed to the yoke and gathered at the bottom, baste it to the right front. Close at the left side with hooks and eyes.

THE BACK

Is faced with the same material as the vest front, and looped up to form a bow in center of back. Any style of trimming may be used.

THE SKIRT

Is laid in box plaits.

Regulate length by the tape measure.

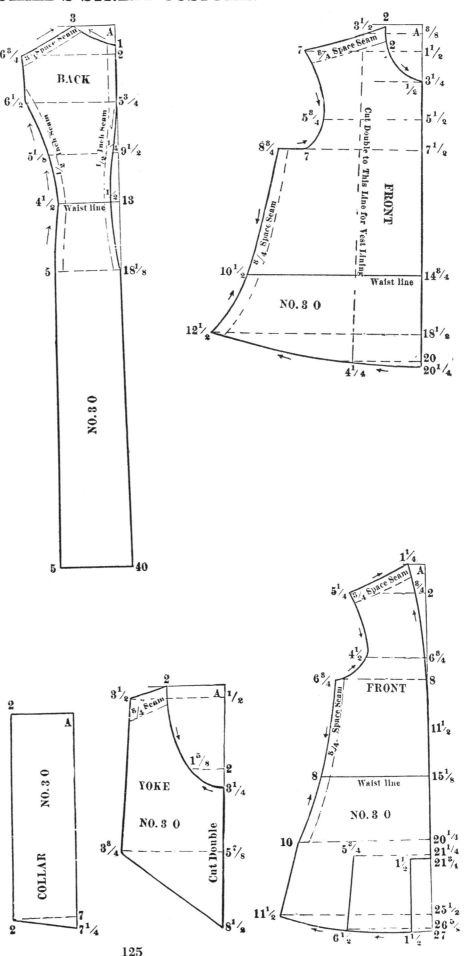

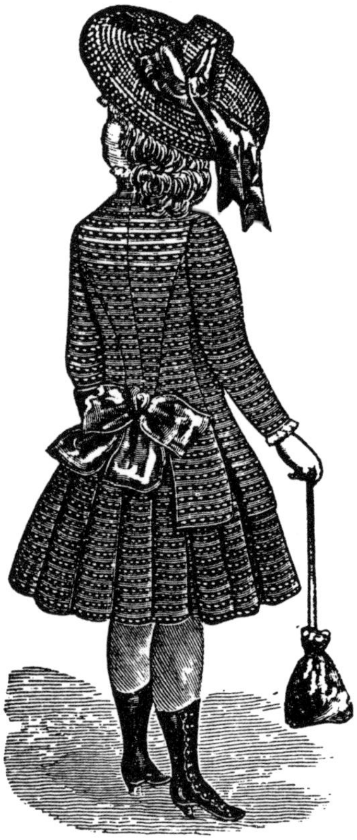

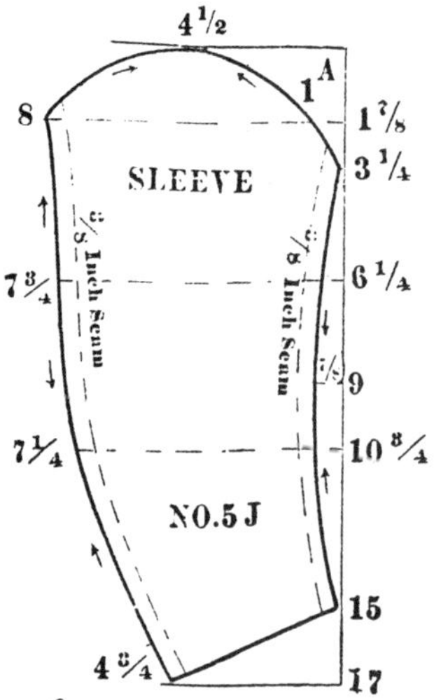
SLEEVE
NO.5 J
3/8 Inch Seam
3/8 Inch Seam

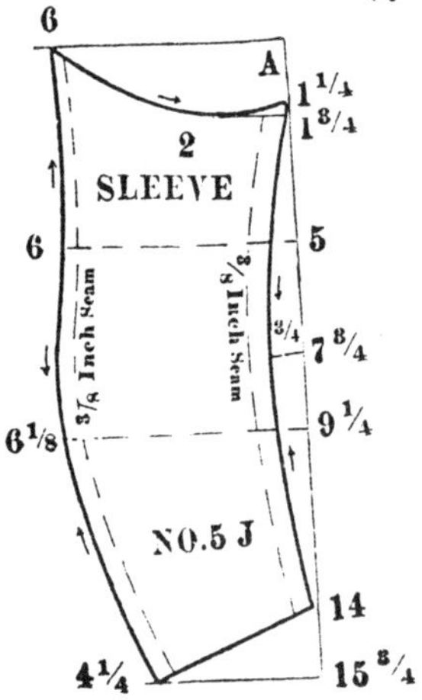
2
SLEEVE
NO.5 J
3/8 Inch Seam
3/8 Inch Seam

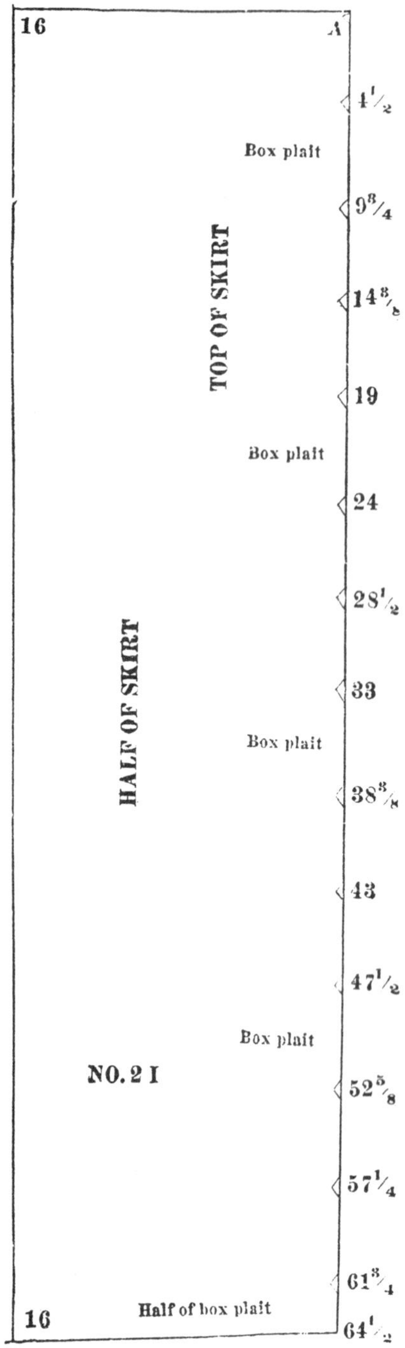
TOP OF SKIRT
HALF OF SKIRT
NO. 2 I
Box plait
Box plait
Box plait
Box plait
Half of box plait

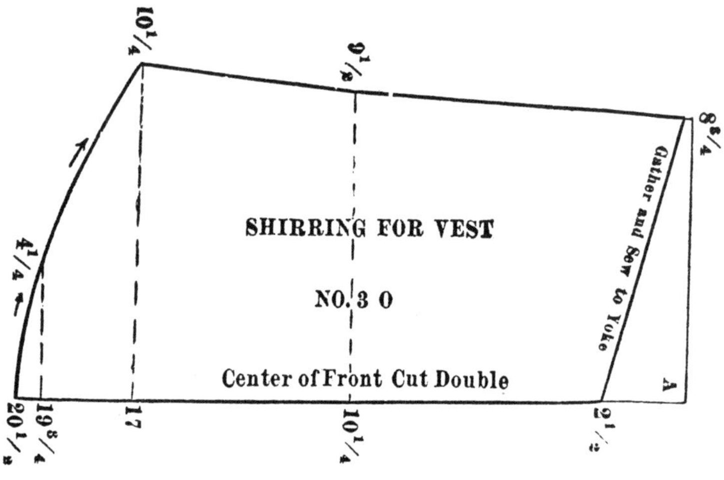
SHIRRING FOR VEST
NO. 3 O
Center of Front Cut Double
Gather and Sew to Yoke

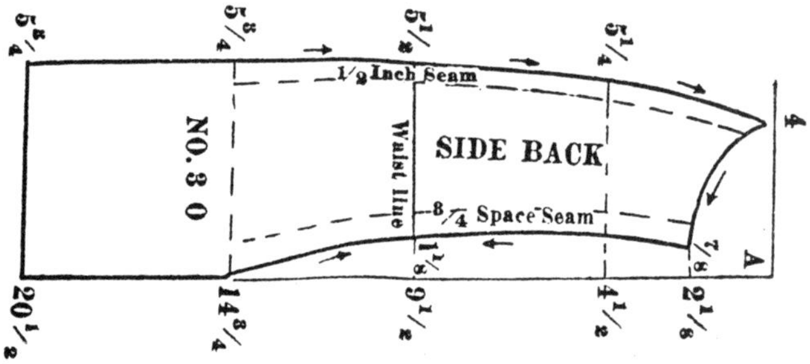
NO. 3 O
SIDE BACK
1/2 Inch Seam
Waist line
3/4 Space Seam

LADIES' COMBINATION UNDERGARMENT.

Use scale corresponding with the bust measure.

Is in three pieces: Front, Back and Sleeve.

Is drafted out upon the general plan of work.

Follow the arrows closely.

No allowance is made for the tucks.

Regulate the length by the use of the tape measure.

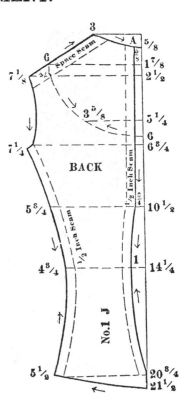

BACK

No.1 J

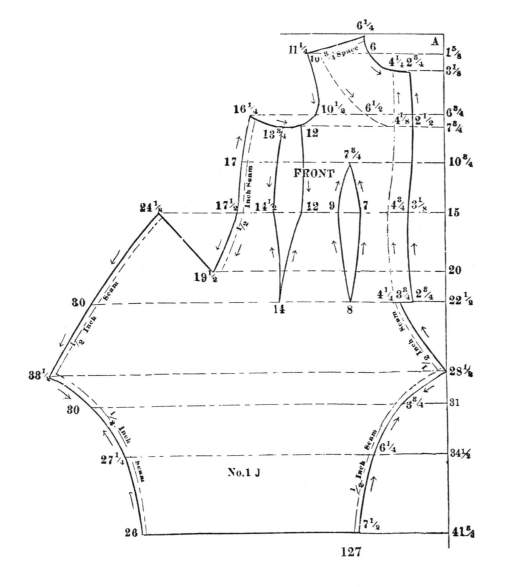

FRONT

No.1 J

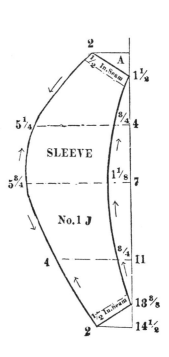

SLEEVE

No.1 J

BOYS' SUIT.

Use scale corresponding with the chest measure.

Is in eight pieces: Front, Back, Collar, Belt and two Sleeve portions, and the two portions for the Knee Pants.

Is drafted on the general plan of work.

Each plait is marked on the draft.

Follow the arrows closely.

THE PANTS

Are drafted by the scale corresponding with the waist measnre.

Regulate the length by the use of the tape measure.

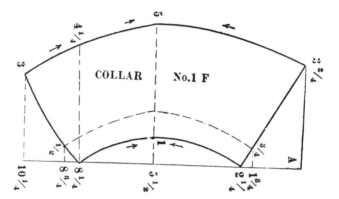

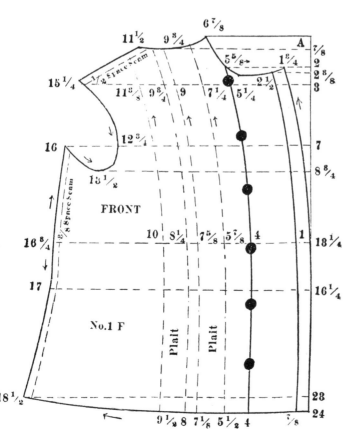

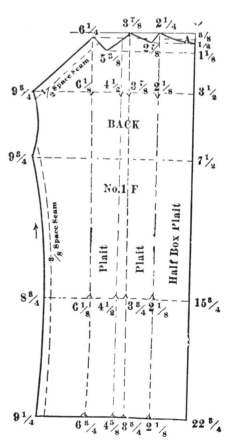

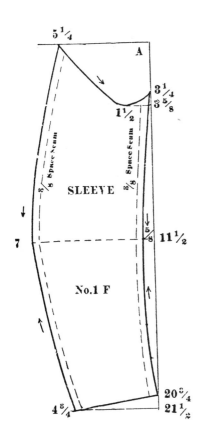

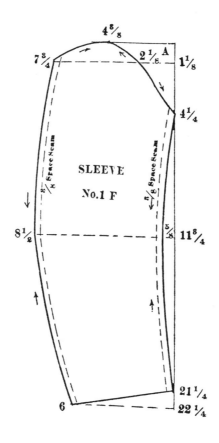

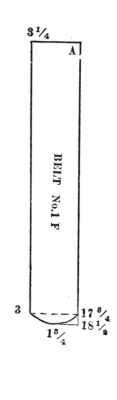

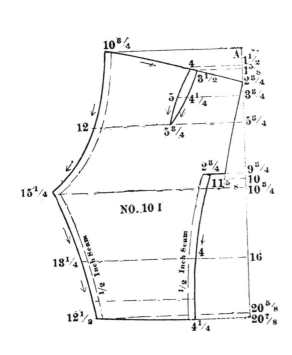

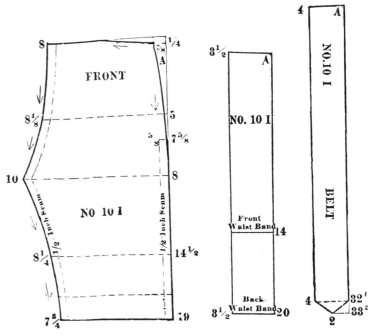

BOYS' SUIT.

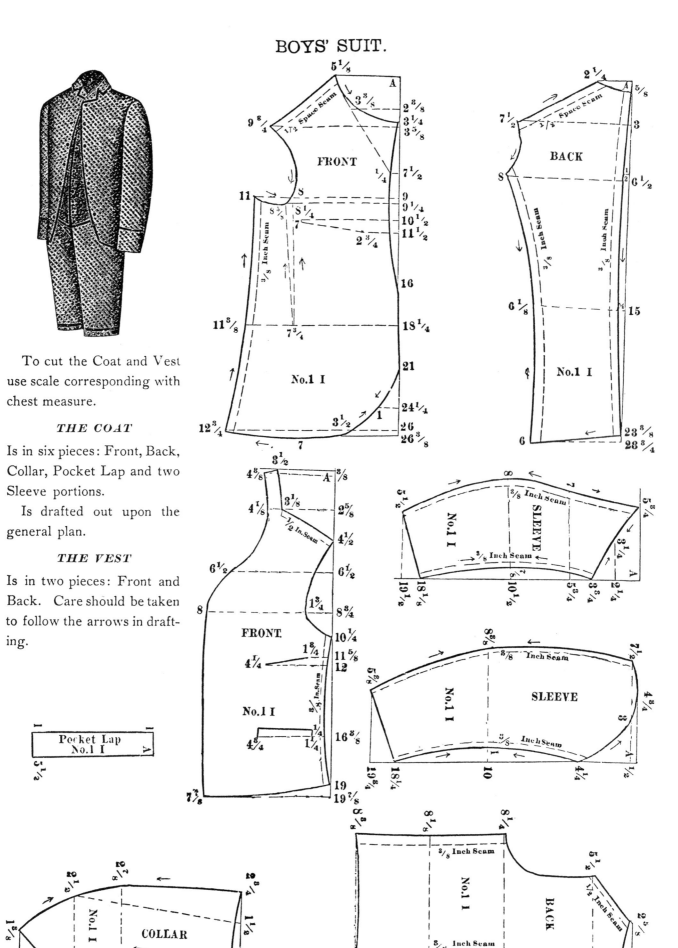

To cut the Coat and Vest use scale corresponding with chest measure.

THE COAT

Is in six pieces: Front, Back, Collar, Pocket Lap and two Sleeve portions.

Is drafted out upon the general plan.

THE VEST

Is in two pieces: Front and Back. Care should be taken to follow the arrows in drafting.

130

MEN'S OVERALLS, WITH APRON

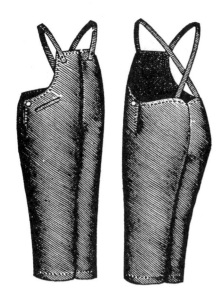

Use scale corresponding with waist measure.

Is in two pieces: one-half of Overalls and Strap.

Regulate the length by the use of the tape line.

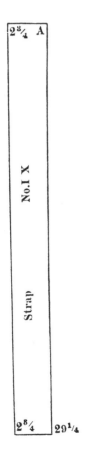

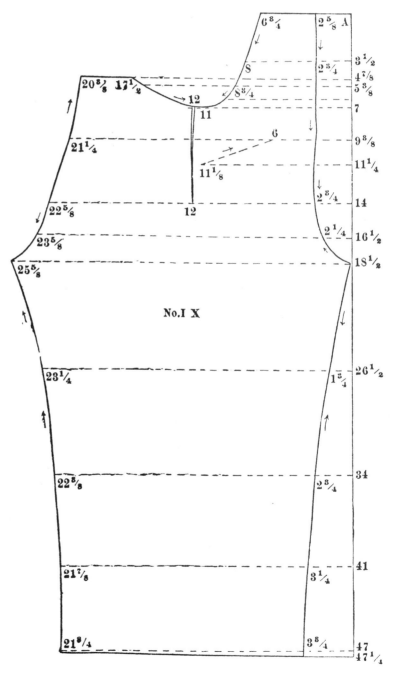

BOYS' OVERCOAT.

Use scale corresponding with bust measure.

Is in seven pieces: Front, Back, Collar, two Pocket Laps and two Sleeve portions.

Is drafted upon the general plan of work.

Regulate the length by the tape measure.

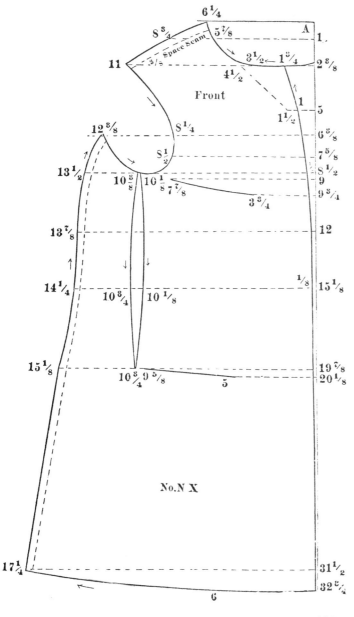

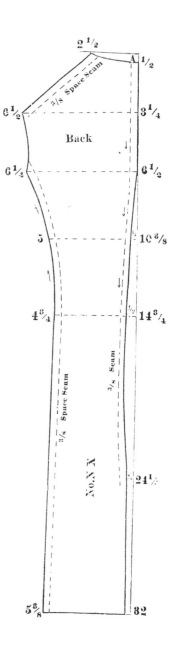

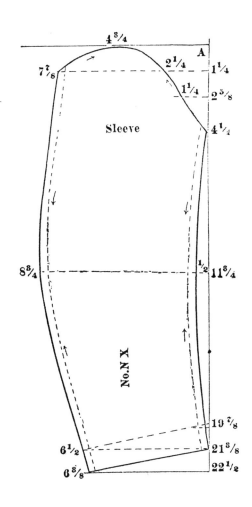

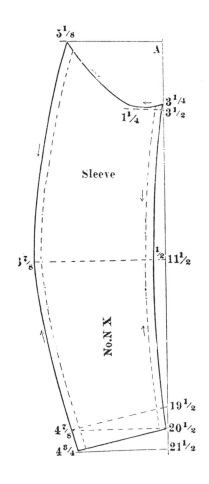

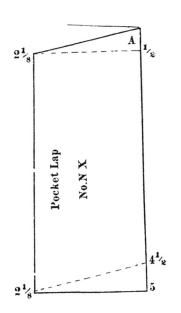

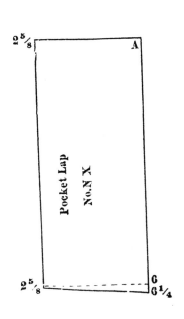

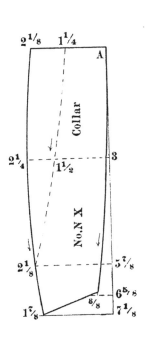

133

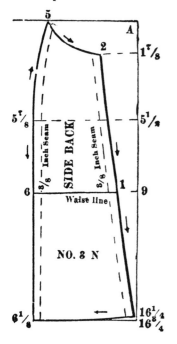

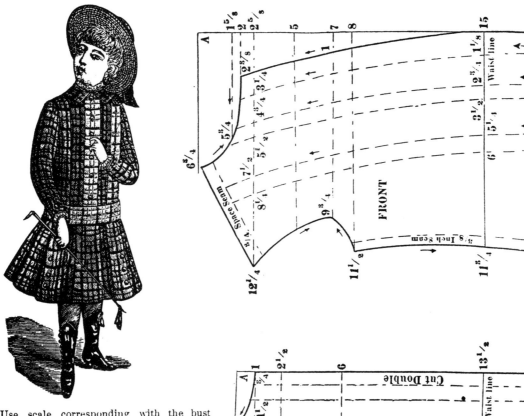

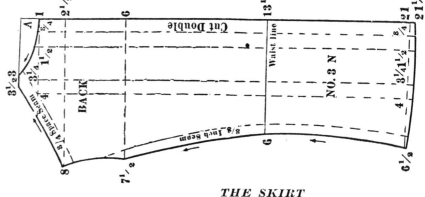

Use scale corresponding with the bust measure.

Is in ten pieces: Front, Back, Side Back, Collar, Cuff, Belt, two Sleeve portions and two portions of the Skirt.

THE FRONT.

Lay a box plait down the center of the front and a side plait on each side turning toward the center of front.

THE BACK.

Lay a box plait down the center of back, and a side plait on each side, turning toward center of back.

Each plait is marked.

THE SKIRT

Is drafted by the waist measure. Is in two pieces: Box Plaiting for front and Side Plaiting for back part of skirt. Each plait is marked. Regulate the length by the tape measure.

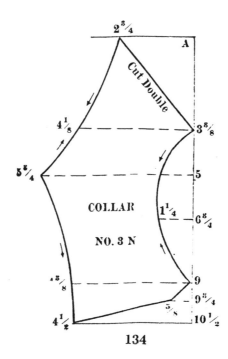

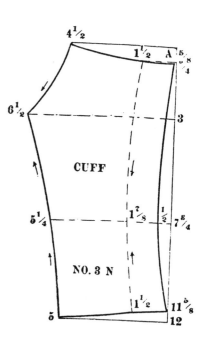

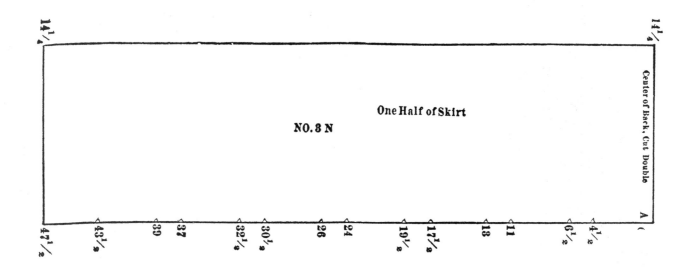

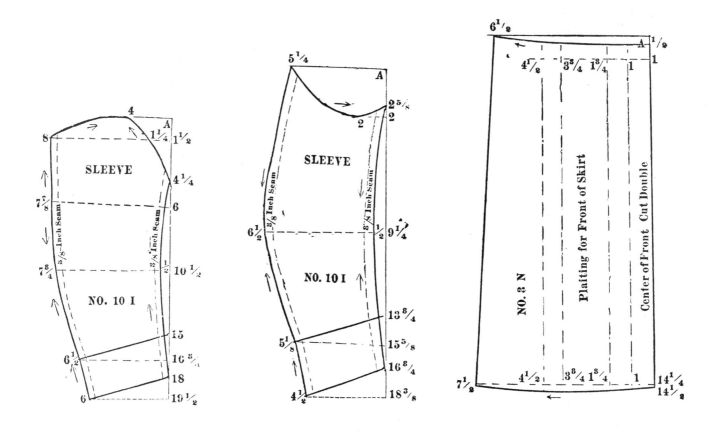

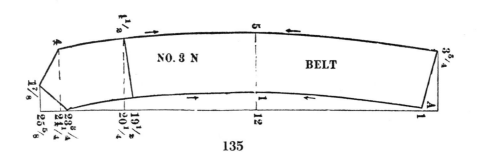

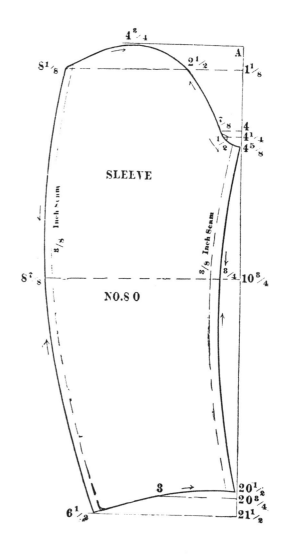

Use scale corresponding with the chest measure. Take the measure over the coat moderately tight. Take sleeve measure from center of back to knuckle joint. Deduct the seams.

This consists of five pieces—Front, Back, Collar, and two Sleeve portions.

The Seams are all ⅜-inch seams.

Regulate the length by the tape measure.

Regulate length and size of waist by tape measure.

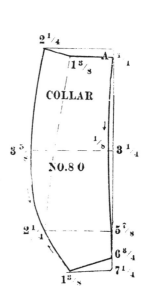

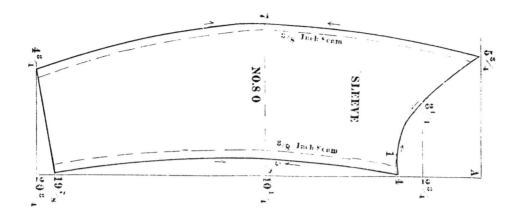

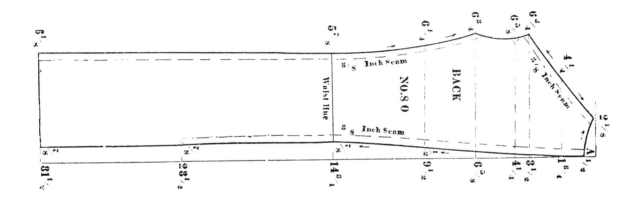

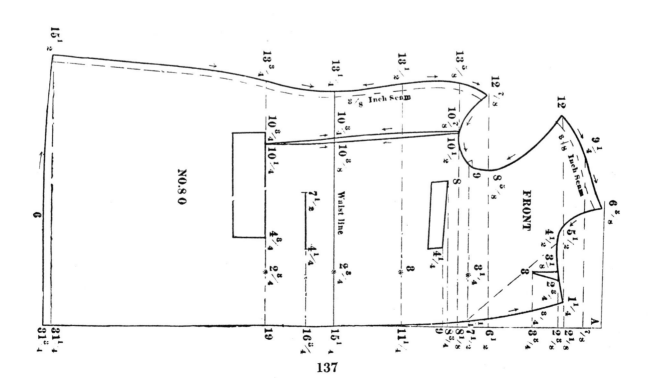

GENTLEMEN'S OVERALLS.

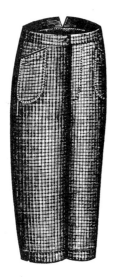

GENTLEMEN'S OVERALLS.

Take the measure directly over the hip to ascertain the number of scale to use. It consists of five pieces: Front, Back, Fly, Strap, and Band. Regulate the length by the tape measure.

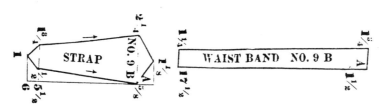

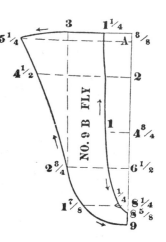

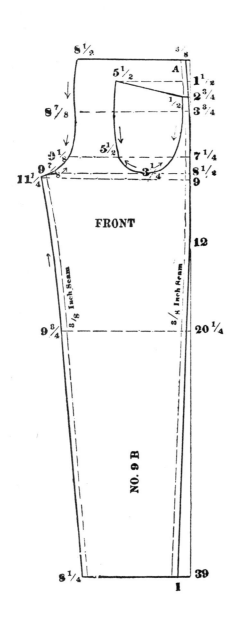

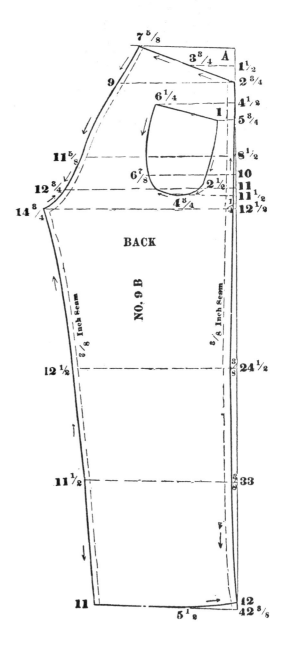

CHILD'S COSTUME.

Draft by chest measure. Only one-half the skirt is given, as both sides are alike.

In making up use half inch seams.

1½ spaces for hem on Vest. Sew Vest on front on line marked on line drawn from 2¾ on top measure line to 4 at the bottom of vest.

Work the button holes in the right side of the vest, sewing buttons on the left side.

There need be no button holes with buttons on either side of vest. If desired, a double row of machine stitching may be used at each side of the front at edge next to vest.

The front in draft is made so as to omit vest, if desired, and make plain front.

If vest is used, cut goods on line marked 1¼ at neck, and 2½ at bottom.

If plain do not cut on this line, but use base line for front edge.

The pocket is merely a strip sewed on, but the pocket can be put in if desired.

Lay a box plait in front of skirt, making the line 61 to 60⅜ from the cut edge of plait, placing this line at 56 at the top, and on the point at 57 at the bottom to form plait. Place 55 on 51¾ at top and 55¼ on 51¾ at the bottom to form next plait; all others are formed in like manner.

Any other style of plaits desired may be used. The skirt is a plain strip of goods length and width desired, and can be cut without draft being made and plaits laid in the goods.

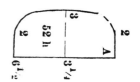

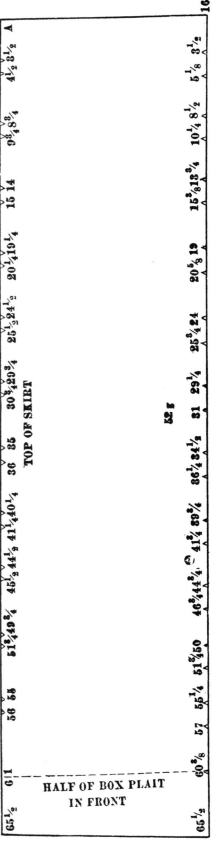

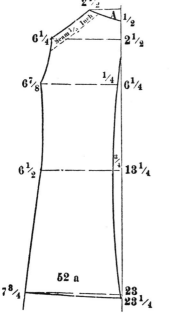

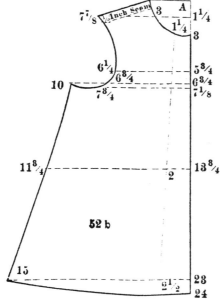

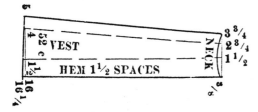

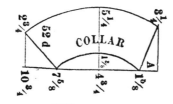

GENTLEMEN'S PRINCE ALBERT COAT.

Use scale corresponding with the chest measure.

Is in eight pieces: Front, Back, Side Back, Skirt, Facing for Front, Collar, and two Sleeve portions.

This is drafted out upon the general plan of work.

Follow the arrows closely.

Regulate the length by the use of the tape measure.

GENTLEMEN'S VEST.

Take the chest measure over the vest and use scale to correspond. Take measure for length from center of the back of the neck over the shoulder, close to the neck, down in front the length to be worn, plus one inch for seams. This will give correct length of vest.

Make up with or without collar, as desired.

The front can be cut higher or lower, to suit.

GENTLEMEN'S PANTS.

Take the measure directly over hip joint—this gives the number of scale to use.

Regulate size of the waist and length of leg by the tape line.

The length of leg can be taken by inseam measure, or from the hip joint to sole of shoe. If the length of the leg has to be changed, change the knee line one-half the distance. Cut the right side of front on the inside line on the front for the fly. Cut the left side on the outer line.

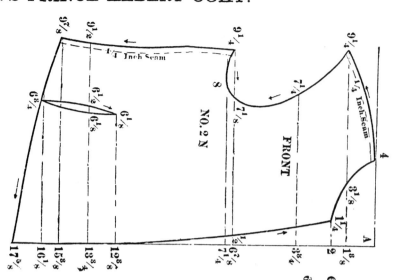

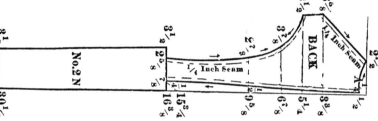

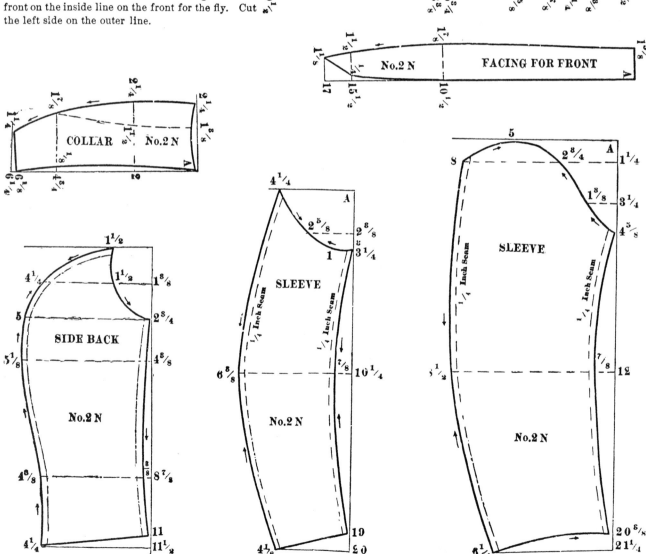

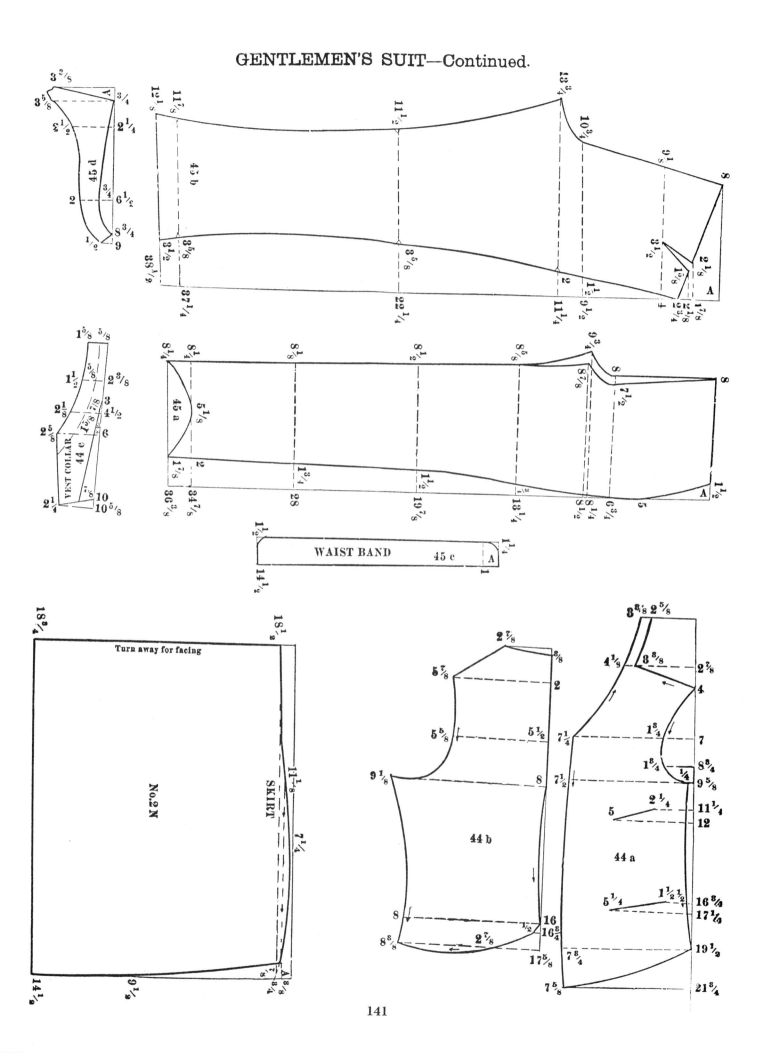

BOYS' OVERCOAT.

Use scale corresponding with the chest measure over the coat.

Is in six pieces: Front, Back, Side Back, Collar, Pocket, Lap and two Sleeve portions.

This garment is drafted upon the general plan of work.

Regulate the length by the tape line.

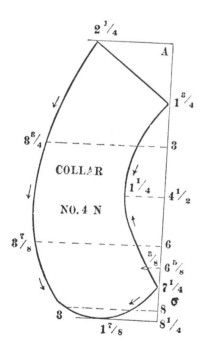

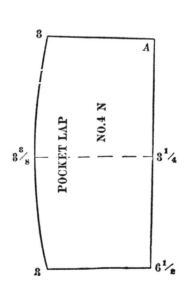

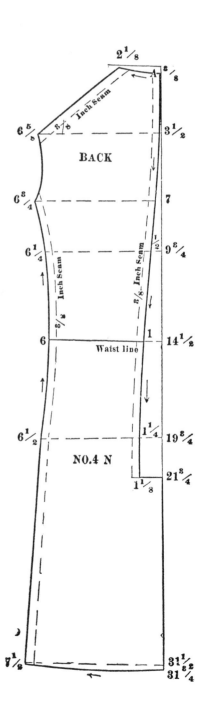

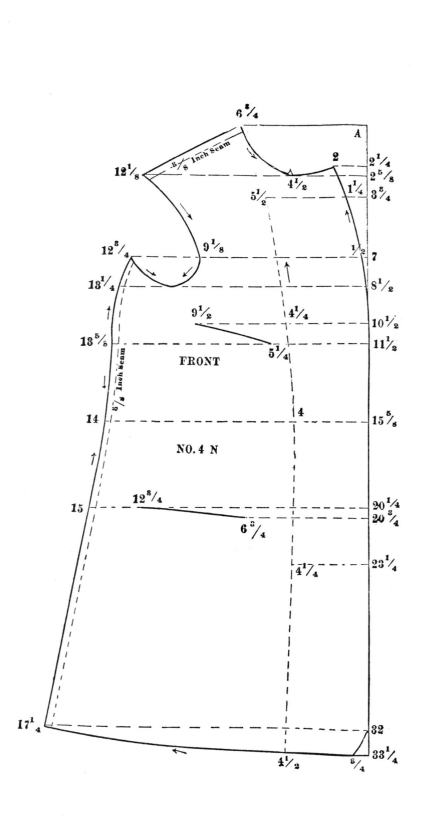

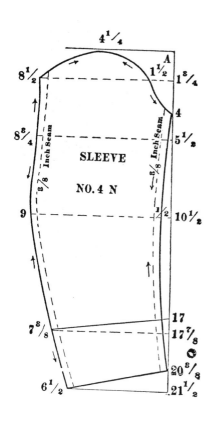

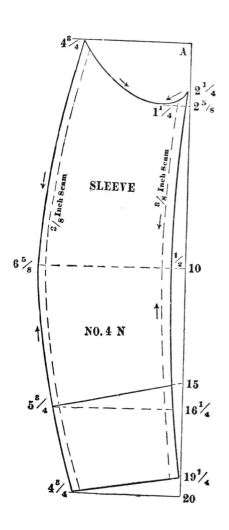

GENTLEMEN'S OVERCOAT.

Draft by scale corresponding with chest measure taken over the coat.

Regulate length and size of waist by tape line.

Take measure for sleeve from center of back to knuckle joint.

Deduct width of back piece—less one inch for seams—this gives length of sleeves. If length of sleeve by the scale corresponds with this measure, the length is correct; if not, change the scale line at wrist until it corresponds with tape measure, changing elbow line one-half the distance same direction. Regulate length to suit.

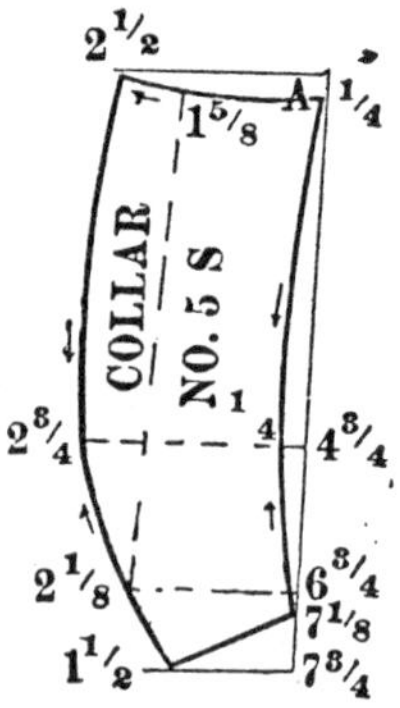

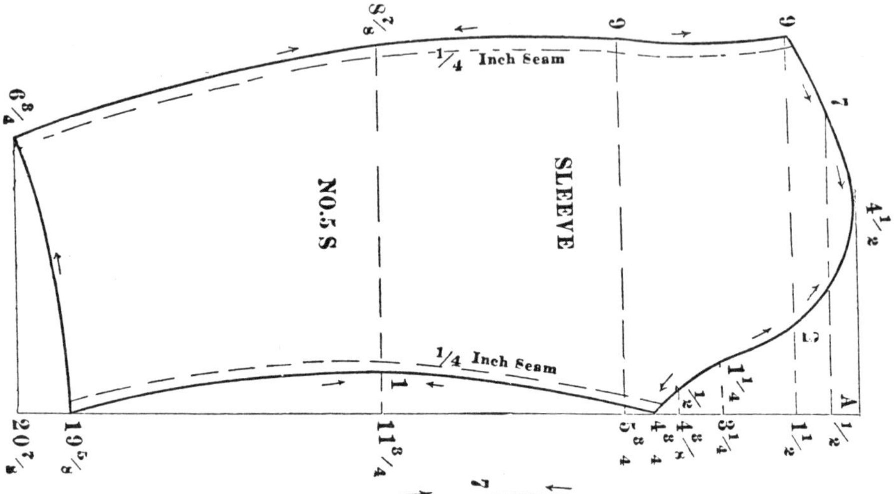

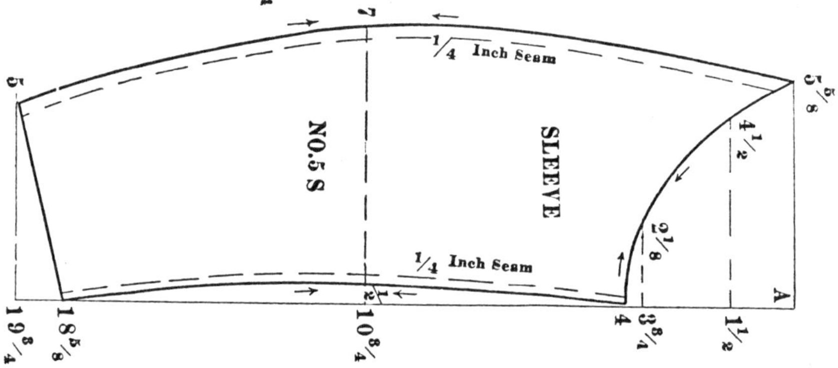

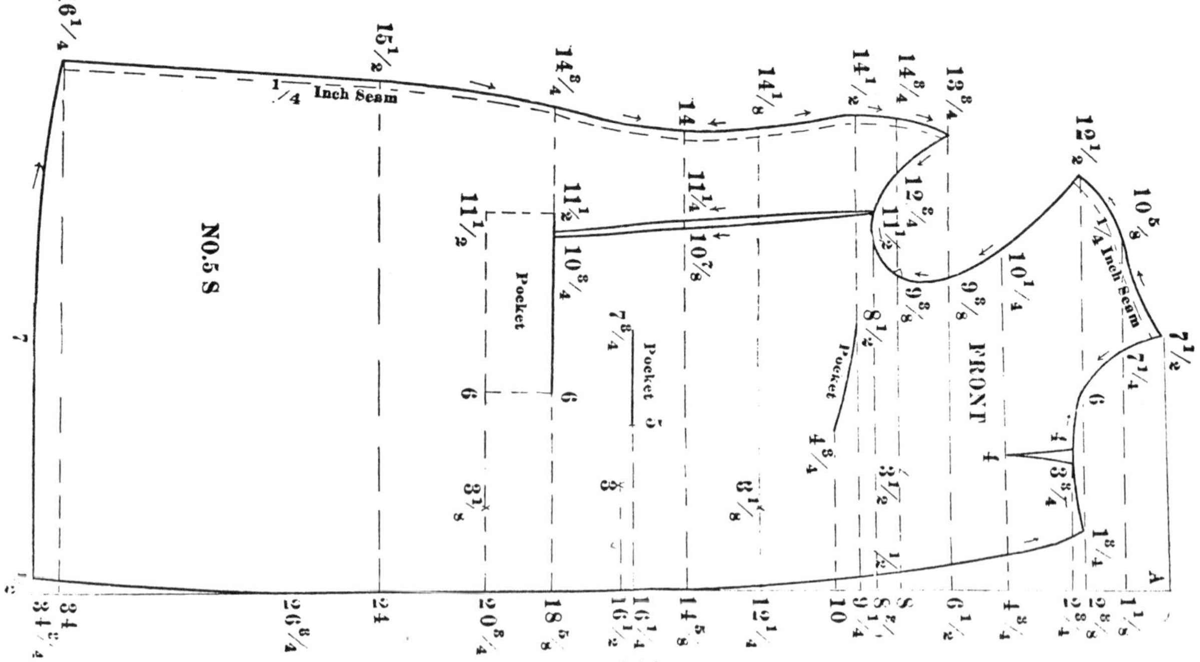

COLLAR NO. 5 S

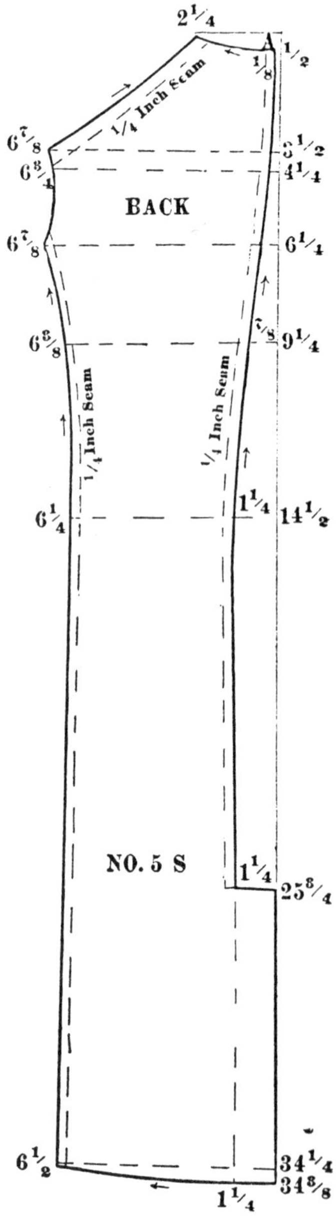

BACK

NO. 5 S

SLEEVE NO. 5 S

SLEEVE NO. 5 S

FRONT

Pocket

NO. 5 S